QUOTABLE ARA

Dad and Mom,

Let this book be one more reminder of what makes Notre Dame so special. I hope you enjoy the book!

Love,

Mike

QUOTABLE ARA

The Words, Wisdom, and Inspiration of Legendary Notre Dame Football Coach Ara Parseghian

Mike Towle

Win-Win Words, LLC
Hendersonville, Tennessee

Thanks to Ara Parseghian, the University of Notre Dame Sports Information Department, University of Notre Dame Media Relations Department, University of Notre Dame Archives, and Northwestern University for their generous assistance with this project.

Cover photo of Ara Parseghian is courtesy of the University of Notre Dame Media Relations Department.

Design by Mike Towle

Printed in the United States of America
1 2 3 4 5 6 — 17 16 15 14 13 12

This book was authorized by Ara Parseghian, and a portion of the proceeds from the sale of this book will be paid to the Ara Parseghian Medical Research Foundation.

Quotable Ara is also available in large-quantity printings as a premium or incentive. Contact publisher Mike Towle at vermonte@bellsouth.net or 615-293-5771 for more information.

CONTENTS

Introduction *vi*

I. Ara: His Own Self 1
II. Ara: Notre Dame Man 7
III. Ara: The Coach 19
IV. Ara: His Players 36
V. Ara: The Motivator 44
VI. Ara: Polls, Bowls, and Big Games 54
VII. Ara: With Feeling 72
VIII. Ara: Keeping It Real 78
IX. Ara: His Humor 83
X. Ara: His Resignation 90
XI. Ara: This and That 98

Ara: Season by Season *103*
Ara: By the Numbers *116*
Resources *125*
The Author *134*

Introduction

Ara Parseghian is not Irish. Neither is he Catholic nor a Notre Dame alum. What he was as a new Notre Dame hire in late 1963 was school president Rev. Theodore Hesburgh's personal pick to revive Notre Dame football. The once-distinguished program had languished for the better part of a decade, beginning after Terry Brennan had replaced Frank Leahy and posted 9-1 and 8-2 records in his first two seasons. In the five seasons directly preceding Parseghian's hiring, the Fighting Irish won 19 games and lost 30 under Joe Kuharich and Hugh Devore, essentially scraping bottom.

After Parseghian arrived in South Bend, he moved players around to different positions. He performed motivational reengineering, turned a benchwarming quarterback into a Heisman Trophy winner and started winning week after week. The rejuvenated Irish under Ara responded in 1964 with a 9-1 season, barely missing out on a perfect 10-0 season, while achieving one of the most astounding turnarounds in college football history. The National Football Foundation awarded Notre Dame with the MacArthur Bowl, long symbolic of the best college football team in the nation.

Parseghian produced winning seasons in each of his eleven years as Notre Dame coach. If there were a Mount Rushmore for Notre Dame football, Parseghian's chiseled bust would be flanked by Knute Rockne and Leahy to his right and by Lou Holtz on his left. Although Rockne and Leahy had slightly gaudier records than Parseghian in terms of winning percentage and undefeated seasons, and while Holtz's gift of gab and one-liners had Rockne and the others trumped, Ara might be the best fit as consummate Notre Dame football coach. He was dashing and personable, creative and daring, relentlessly intense and unquenchably driven to success, yet a charismatic ambassador for the school, a hit on the banquet circuit, and an engagingly candid interview with the media.

A one-time navy man, Ara was a seasoned leader of men long before he took up residence in South Bend. Not only did he have fourteen years of college coaching under his belt, he had also played college ball and a year-plus of pro football, along the way soaking up football ingenuity from the coaching braniac likes of Woody Hayes, Sid Gillman, and Paul Brown. Parseghian had a knack for matching players to positions, could discern how to motivate a melting pot of talent and could see things in X's and O's that most others failed to interpolate. "He was a visionary," long-time assistant Tom Pagna said.

Ara was 95-17-4 (.836) in eleven seasons at Notre Dame. His teams lost more than two games in a season just once (8-3 in 1972), and the number of times his Irish lost a game by 20 or more points can be counted on one hand—four, out of 116 games played. Notre Dame won two official national titles, each accompanied by undefeated records under Parseghian, and only two of his eleven teams finished outside the Associated Press's final Top 10, although both those teams were still ranked in the top 15.

When Parseghian stepped down as Notre Dame football coach in 1974, to be replaced by Dan Devine, it was speculated Ara would stay out of coaching for a short sabbatical and then return to the sideline, presumably in the National Football League. He was only fifty-one years old, less than twelve months removed from his second national title. Health concerns drove Ara from the game he loved at the prime of his career. For Parseghian, the warning signs were sleepless nights and prescriptions for high blood pressure. His doctor told him it was time to get out of coaching; either that or the stress could soon kill him. So he got out, never to return to coaching.

The essence of Parseghian's timeless wit, wisdom, and inspiration contained in this book includes more than 250 of his most insightful and memorable quotes gleaned from more than fifty years' worth of published works. These date back to his days as a head coach at Miami (Ohio) University and continuing through his years at Northwestern, Notre Dame, and beyond, to include a smattering of additional insights he offered during an interview conducted especially for this book.

Brought together into this one volume, Ara Parseghian's words not only examine the world of college football and peel away the layers of Notre Dame's mystique, but also offer dozens of success principles suitable for locker rooms and board rooms.

QUOTABLE ARA

I
Ara: His Own Self

She wanted a girl, and I wasn't a girl.[1]

— referring to his mother, Amelia, who often dressed Ara in girl's clothes the first two years of his life until his sister was born

ARA WAS A REAL GOOD BOY. WE HAD VERY LITTLE TROUBLE WITH HIM.[2]

— Amelia Parseghian

ONCE THE TEACHER SENT HOME A NOTE ABOUT ARA. SHE SAID HE WAS A BRIGHT BOY, BUT HIS MIND ALWAYS SEEMED ON SOMETHING ELSE. I KNOW WHAT IT WAS—PLAYING BALL.[3]

— Amelia Parseghian

THE BOARD OF EDUCATION WAS HAVING A LOT OF TROUBLE WITH VANDALS BREAKING WINDOWS. SO THEY JUST HIRED ARA TO PATROL THE GROUNDS. THE CHECKS CAME DIRECTLY FROM THE BOARD OF EDUCATION. HE WAS REAL PROUD OF THAT.[4]

— Gerald Parseghian, Ara's brother, remembering when Ara was an eighth grader and voted toughest kid in school

My life's experience has taught me one thing well. Never try to imitate or envy anyone. Always be yourself.[5]

I have this tendency to leave good things and go on to other things that are attractive—that are attractive, I guess, because they are so tough.[6]

I have never smoked. Well, I'll take that back. I was on the road a lot one winter, making speeches, and I found that a cigar kept me awake on the long drives home. Sort of whetted my energy. But I gave them up, too.[7]

I have to keep moving.[8]

I have never seen my daughter more radiant than (when) she was coming back out of the church that night. She had made it.[9]

— recalling the wedding of his daughter Karan, who had been diagnosed with multiple sclerosis sometime earlier

How in the heavens do you know that?[10]

Let me assure you, my sense of fair play would acknowledge the violation and pay the fine without protest if I were guilty.[11]

— from a note he sent to court officials after he was cited for speeding near his Marco Island winter home in Florida. Parseghian, clocked at 73 in a 55 zone, was passing a slow-moving van as he sped up to avoid an oncoming car.

If you are not grateful for the people who help you, you are not a person.[12]

Every minute wasted is a minute lost forever.[13]

I don't worry about the past. I can't tell you what I had for breakfast yesterday.[14]

I've always realized that nothing is older than yesterday's newspaper. I keep things in perspective. I'm comfortable with myself.[15]

Make your children get involved, whether it's football, band, debating, or any other activity. Discipline and teamwork apply in almost every activity of your life.[16]

The religion point came up in my Notre Dame interview. I found Notre Dame to be broad-minded in this respect. I expected to see nothing but priests. I found they made up only 15 percent of the faculty. The rest are lay people—including Jews and Protestants. I feel perfectly at home in South Bend.[17]

— *Parseghian is Presbyterian*

The Parseghian family after the move to Notre Dame in 1964. Kristan, 12, and Mike, 9, in front; daughter Karan, 14, wife Katie, and Ara in back. Courtesy of University of Notre Dame Media Relations Department.

THEY TOLD US HE WAS ANOTHER ROCKNE. THE NERVE OF THEM. WHY, I CHECKED PERSONALLY AND HIS NOSE WAS STRAIGHT, HE HAD ALL HIS HAIR, AND HE DOESN'T SPEAK LIKE A GATLING GUN. HE DOESN'T WEAR HATS THAT LOOK LIKE HE FOUND THEM UNDER A TRUCK. ARA WOULD HAVE TO STAY IN MAKEUP FOR TWO DAYS TO LOOK AS BAD AS ROCK.[18]

— ***sports columnist Jim Murray***

Hey, how long is this going to take? I've gotta get a haircut.[19]

— cutting short a telephone interview with a reporter

II
Ara: Notre Dame Man

WE HAVE COME HERE TODAY TO HIRE ARA PARSEGHIAN. NOW SHOW ME THE VOTE.[1]

— *Rev. Theodore Hesburgh to the school's athletic board, after the* South Bend Tribune *reported that Parseghian was being hired as Notre Dame coach, in December 1963*

WE HAD TO GO FOR THE BEST MAN AVAILABLE. WE HAD TO PICK AN AMBITIOUS YOUNG MAN WHO ALREADY HAD PROVEN HE COULD WIN IN THE KIND OF COMPETITION WE MEET.[2]

— *Hesburgh, upon hiring Parseghian*

I REGRET THAT WE HAVE NO STATEMENT AT THIS TIME, BUT MR. PARSEGHIAN STATED EARLIER TODAY WE EXPECT TO RESOLVE OUR DIFFICULTIES WITHIN A DAY OR TWO.[3]

— statement by Rev. Edmund P. Joyce, Notre Dame executive vice president, after Parseghian walked out before a press conference announcing him as new Notre Dame coach

All hell busted loose when I walked out, and I realized the scope of coaching at Notre Dame. Man, you cough in your office and everybody in the world knows you got pneumonia.[4]

PARSEGHIAN SHOULD BE HERE A LONG TIME. HE TOOK THE JOB TWICE.[5]

— Edward "Moose" Krause, Notre Dame athletic director

(Father Hesburgh) told me just one thing when I came here. He told me, "I don't care if you go 5-5 every year as long as you run an honest program. But if you go 10-0 and cheat, you're gone."[6]

I DON'T UNDERSTAND WHY ARA IS LEAVING THE BIG TEN. BUT IT MUST BE OKAY, BECAUSE ARA IS TERRIBLY EXCITED ABOUT GOING TO NOTRE DAME.[7]

— Amelia Parseghian, Ara's mom

Notre Dame was an opportunity that presented itself at the right time; there are often some doors of opportunity ajar that you can nudge a little bit.[8]

When twenty-five hundred students showed up, singing, "Cheer, cheer for old Notre Dame" in cold and a foot of snow, I knew the coach here indeed has something extra special going for him.[9]

The restoration of Notre Dame's football image is my main objective. I hope . . . I think . . . that it can be done within four years.[10]

I am not deaf and I am not naïve. The students think this will be a new era for Notre Dame football . . . and they are right. I am determined it will be a winning era.[11]

ARA, STOP THE SNOW! ARA, STOP THE SNOW![12]

— ***Notre Dame students pleading their confidence in Parseghian when a snowstorm hit during a game against Navy***

Even at Notre Dame we had to dress in the old stadium at first. We had virtually no weight room. Weights weren't that big a deal. We had no indoor facility whatsoever.[13]

Knute Rockne is more alive around here today than a lot of live people somewhere else.[14]

I say college football began with Rockne.[15]

All teams have peaks and valleys as far as talent is concerned. And Notre Dame had had a few lost years just before I came. They were hungry. It was timing—and putting the right players in the right positions and having assistants to get the most out of them.[16]

A trip to a bowl may be attractive to the players of many teams, but because Notre Dame already plays a nationwide schedule that takes us from coast to coast, there is no real need of an intersectional trip. The ten-game schedule played by Notre Dame is long enough for any team from the "snow belt" where outdoor practice in the late fall can be a real problem.[17]

— justifying in 1966 Notre Dame's no-bowl policy, which was changed just three years after this statement

NOTRE DAME DID PLAY A BOWL GAME IN 1925. WE WILL NOT PLAY ANOTHER. WHY NOT? BECAUSE, AS FAR AS OUR STUDENTS ARE CONCERNED, WE KNOW THAT THEY CANNOT BE ENGAGED IN AS EXCITING A PURSUIT AS FOOTBALL FOR THREE QUARTERS OF A SEMESTER AND STILL MAINTAIN A 77-PERCENT AVERAGE. IF THEY DO NOT HAVE THE REQUIRED AVERAGE, EITHER THEY DO NOT PLAY THE NEXT YEAR, OR WE LOWER OUR STANDARDS, AND THEN THEY STOP GETTING DIPLOMAS.[18]

— Rev. Theodore Hesburgh, who was Notre Dame president during the Ara years at Notre Dame

At Notre Dame every game is a bowl game. We are on a semester basis, and we feel it would interfere with our classroom program. A ten-game season is long enough.[19]

Whether you like it or not, ... you're a national figure after five games at Notre Dame.[20]

If you make a mistake in business, you can hide it in a desk drawer where nobody sees it.[21]

There's no middle ground with Notre Dame. People either love us or hate us. My own brother's best friend, a Michigan alumnus, once said to me, "I have two favorite teams—Michigan and whoever is playing Notre Dame."[22]

When a boy comes to Notre Dame, he has to know he won't be used. So he believes in us, and we believe in him. And that's what gives us all a sense of unity, spirit, and responsibility.[23]

ARA Q&A

Q: *Four years after Father Hesburgh wrote in an essay that Notre Dame would never go to a bowl game, Notre Dame accepted a bid to the 1970 Cotton Bowl to play Texas. What changed?*

A: My first year there, there was some tentative bowl talk, but it was squelched in a hurry. Father Joyce was in favor of it overall, but he didn't have the kind of influence needed to win over Father Hesburgh, who was pretty adamant back in those days. Then in 1966, we had another situation that revived bowl talk. The late-season collision between Michigan State and Notre Dame was looming, and you could see where either of these teams might still be in position after the game to go to a bowl game with an opportunity to win the national championship. So there were some bowl discussions that fall, too. I think Father Joyce believed he had Father Hesburgh's ear, but it didn't turn out.

Then in 1969, there was again some discussion, a lot of it in fact, about Notre Dame going to a bowl. This was a period when money was a little tight. Father Joyce worked on Father Hesburgh on this issue and finally got him moving in the right direction, with the idea that there would be four parameters used to

Ara talks with bowl officials while flanked by Notre Dame President Rev. Ted Hesburgh (left) and University Executive Vice-President Rev. Edmund P. Joyce (right). University of Notre Dame Archives.

determine whether or not we would go to a bowl game. This included if the bowl involved a national championship or paired us against a team ranked above us so we could improve our position. What it boiled down to was money and minority scholarships. Father Hesburgh had been involved with a number of governmental programs and committees related to minority improvement. I'm guessing in his own mind he was influenced by how the bowl money could be directed toward academic scholarships.

As many advantages as there are to coaching at Notre Dame, one of the difficult things about coaching there was that we didn't belong to a conference or go to bowl games. We couldn't afford to lose a game because then we couldn't expect any kind of high national ranking. So winning was VERY important to us, where a team in a conference can lose a conference game but still go on to win the conference title and then go to a bowl game. It always bothered me because I knew we didn't have any option. We had a ten-game schedule and that was it. Just like in 1966 when we played Michigan State to the 10-10 tie, leaving No. 1 still in doubt. We didn't have a bowl game after that, although what happened to work out for us is that we still had one more game to play, against Southern Cal. We overwhelmed them, and that made a difference in our winning the national championship.

I'm under intense pressure to win football games and keep my program going, but I feel like a teacher and an educator, too. It's a good, wholesome experience. I like to be around an academic community such as the one at Notre Dame—the culture, the arts.[24]

May the image cast by this mirror forever reflect the honor and the glory of a Notre Dame man.[25]

— inscription on back of mirror on Notre Dame office desk

It won't be long before Notre Dame is recognized as the leading Presbyterian university in the Midwest.[26]

— joking when told Knute Rockne arrived at Notre Dame a Protestant but was buried a Catholic

I'm flattered that my name comes up in job discussions. But sometimes I think that people bring it up just to complicate my relationship at Notre Dame. Every time I'm linked with a job, I have to reassure the school, my staff, the players, and even potential prospects.[27]

That's the penalty of coaching and playing at Notre Dame. Everybody thinks we're invincible at home.[28]

There is absolutely no pressure on me from the administration to win. The only pressures on me are self-inflicted. They come from my own pride, my desire to be successful.[29]

When I was at Northwestern, there was pressure because the Big Ten was well-recognized as the premier conference in the entire United States. But there was no way I could even imagine the responsibility of being the Notre Dame coach until I arrived on campus and came to learn it.[30]

At Northwestern, we played Notre Dame, but we were only on the Notre Dame campus for one day when we played in South Bend; we came, we played a game, we went home. The only way to experience the pressure is to sit in the coach's chair and wear the coach's shoes, then you'll totally understand all the ramifications, the responsibilities, the demands on your time.[31]

You know what I'm most proud of? I'm proudest of the fact that I've been the coach here for ten years. That means I was good enough to do the job, that I met the Notre Dame challenge.[32]

You become a victim of your own success.[33]

I'd like to see the next person who lasts eleven seasons on the job. It's difficult to tell somebody what to expect as the Notre Dame head coach. Sure, there's pressure at Ohio State and Alabama, but it mostly extends from the borders of each state. At Notre Dame, the pressure extends from coast to coast, maybe across the oceans. It is the Catholic university in the country, and you know how many Catholics there are out there.[34]

— as of 2011 only one coach (Lou Holtz, 1986-96) had lasted long enough to match Ara's tenure of eleven seasons

III
Ara: The Coach

Anyone who would get into coaching has got to be nuts.[1]

— *spoken as his playing days in pro football were ending*

It's quite conceivable that I could have become a basketball coach if that job had opened first![2]

— *looking back on his days coaching both freshman football and basketball at Miami (Ohio), where he was told that he was next in line for the varsity head-coaching job for whichever one came open first. Football came first, when Woody Hayes left Miami to go to Ohio State*

Good coaches are very special people who exert a great influence on young athletes, more so than teachers, more so than Dad, more so than anyone. That is a sweeping statement, but the implications are obvious for all who are called, "Coach."[3]

I think a coach must be himself. I'm the yelling and hollering type, so I yell and holler. Whether I'm gloomy or happy, I show how I actually feel. That's my nature.[4]

I've looked back and asked myself why it was that way. I realized that I wouldn't have had the success I did without doing it that way. That's just the way my personality was.[5]

— on his year-round emotional intensity and many near-sleepless nights as Notre Dame coach

I can't hold back. I'm the kind of guy that likes to shoot from the shoulder.[6]

Coaching for me is not really work as a labor, but a physical and mental enjoyment.[7]

I can't coach from a tower. I must be in the huddle. I must be on the line. I must be in the action.[8]

The worst seat in the house is on the sidelines.[9]

— referring to how difficult it is to follow the action from a field-level perspective

TO ALL THE YOUNG GIRLS WHO THINK IT WOULD BE EXCITING TO MARRY A FOOTBALL COACH, I SAY, PICK ONE WHO IS INTELLIGENT, PERSONABLE, ENTHUSIASTIC, AND LUCKY. IT TAKES A LITTLE OF ALL THESE THINGS TO SURVIVE THE WHIMS OF AN ELUSIVE LITTLE BALL AND THE SKILLS AND EMOTIONS OF A GROUP OF YOUNG MEN. AND, EVEN WITH THE BEST, YOU WILL HAVE ROUGH DAYS.[10]

— Katie Parseghian, Ara's wife

I like coaching in college because I enjoy dealing with players who are in the age bracket where they are impressionable.[11]

A coach has to be a chaplain, a public relations man, a disciplinarian, a counselor, an educator. But I like that. I like it a lot.[12]

I can't take credit for producing the God-given innate skills of my football players. I take credit only for recognizing their ability. We've only refined their techniques.[13]

I had experience at virtually every position except end. That came in very handy later on when I became a coach. I had a feel for just what each of those positions required.[14]

— *referring to his having played offensive guard, center, defensive lineman, fullback, and linebacker while in high school, then halfback and defensive back in college*

Some coaches cannot look at their players and instinctively feel where to position them. Some have outstanding players sitting on the bench. . . . Some have people playing defense who should be quarterbacks. . . . It's the coach's ability to condition it, refine it, and put all the right pieces in the proper places that makes the machine go.[15]

We know that even our families, our wives, don't really appreciate what makes us do it. We try to put it into words, but when we do it, it comes out sounding illogical for anybody to stay in such a line of work.[16]

ARA Q&A

Q: *Over eleven seasons at Notre Dame, your teams won 83.6 percent of their games; that's just seventeen losses in eleven years. A record like that suggests a consistently peak performance from week to week, getting up for all the "big" games and avoiding letdowns much of the rest of the time. What's your secret?*

A: I would evaluate the previous game on Sunday. By Monday I had developed the motivation and the reasonings for the upcoming game. I used history; I used the past game; I used the season; a number of things, and I would list all these key points in order of importance. I would try to point out to the team that next Saturday's game would not be won on last Saturday's performance. You can't be hanging onto a win for too long because somebody is getting ready to knock your block off. I generally had what I call my bible containing all the stuff that was important, and I had a folder for every game.

A couple years ago I went back and looked at some of that stuff, and saw where I had written stuff down and started talking about these key points at Monday's practice, and it was different each week. I had a card in my hand where I had jotted down a few words that I would refer to and which would trigger exactly what I wanted to say. I presented it very businesslike: "This is what we've got this week. This is the challenge we have," and during the course of the week I would give them jabs pointing out to them how they were practicing.

The coaching technique that I adopted was Paul Brown's. You start them out with the basic stuff early in the week, work them hard in the middle, then taper off before the game. Mentally, you explain to them early in the week the what, the who and the why, and what we have to do. We hit on Tuesday and Wednesday, and our Thursday practice was an hour and fifteen minutes. We had rehearsal on Friday. You didn't want to peak too soon.

HE WAS A VISIONARY.[17]

— *Tom Pagna, on Ara*

It's much tougher to evaluate talent in the collegiate ranks than in the pros because you do not know what you'll have each year, and you must do what your personnel dictates.[18]

I don't think you should copy somebody exactly. You learn from them how to do it, then adjust it to how you can do it best as an individual.[19]

— referring to the influence that legendary coach Paul Brown and others had on him

I think coaches are interested in winning games, not running up the score.[20]

There is no question about my policy on runaways, and there is a definite pattern to our second-half actions. Go all out the first half, then let the second-, third-, and fourth-stringers play when the game is in your control. Keep the ball on the ground, and use basic defenses.[21]

— excerpt from a seven-page letter he wrote to Miami Herald *sports writer Edwin Pope, rebutting charges by Pope that he had run up the score on outmanned opponents while at Notre Dame*

I know when I talk with a high school coach it doesn't take me long to get a feel for his interests, knowledge, and enthusiasm; what kind of motivator he is, how technique-conscious he is. These are the things that impress a college coach even more than wins and losses.[22]

I constantly look for information, and any one point may stimulate you into another profitable channel to solve some problem in the future. Ideas filter through.[23]

— on visiting other schools and attending coaching clinics

ARA WAS A GREAT TEACHER AND A GREAT COMMUNICATOR. ARA WAS ALSO A LEADER. HE HAD BEEN IN THE NAVY AND HAD MEN UNDER HIM. HE UNDERSTOOD THAT DEFENSE WAS THE MOST IMPORTANT THING IN FOOTBALL. AND HE KNEW BOTH SIDES OF THE BALL VERY WELL. IT'S RARE TO FIND ALL THOSE QUALITIES IN ONE PERSON.[24]

— Tom Pagna

I think a coach will last longer if he can spread out some of the responsibilities—including fundraising, recruiting, and the day-to-day problems like academics, the kids' personal problems, staff problems, and the administration. It's a very demanding job.[25]

I couldn't live with myself if I was a loser, any more than I could live with myself if I had to cheat to win.[26]

It's one thing to lose football games and another thing not to know why.[27]

Failures in coaching have many reasons, and all of them are painful enough when they lead to a loss. But for a coach to be beaten in his strategy is the most embarrassing loss of all.[28]

I don't care how much football my coaching staff knows. I want to know if there's loyalty in the group.[29]

I've been accused of being lucky at times during my coaching career; but, gee, I'd much rather be lucky than good any day.[30]

I would agree that the next level for me is pro football in the event I get itchy feet again.[31]

I have absolutely no intention of becoming a pro football coach. Maybe it would enhance our chances (against Texas) if I said I was. But don't tell the squad that.[32]

— before beating Texas in the 1971 Cotton Bowl

I knew if I took an NFL job, I would be going into a big city, and I didn't know if I wanted that.[33]

I want you to throw everything at them but the kitchen sink. I want them to be ready for everything when it comes time to play the game.[34]

— to his assistants in 1964, his first season at Notre Dame

Purdue is next up at Notre Dame Stadium. Better get there early to beat the crowd.[35]

— after a season-opening 31-7 victory over Wisconsin to begin the magical 1964 turnaround season

Everyone who knows me realizes that I like the passing game in college football. It has been the spectators' delight ever since Gus Dorais started a new trend in football with his passes to Knute Rockne in 1913.[36]

Back in my last year of coaching, it was unusual to encounter three or four outstanding passers in our eleven-game schedule. Today, almost every major team has a tremendous passer. And defensive coaches have to build upon what they already have in order to stop whatever fad is in vogue.[37]

If I hadn't had the head-coaching pressures until later, I may have lasted five or ten more years, who knows?[38]

— *spoken in light of the fact that he spent just one year as an assistant coach before becoming a head coach at age 28*

TWO OF THE BIGGEST THINGS HE DID WERE THAT HE GOT MORE INVOLVED IN RECRUITING, AND HE ANALYZED EVERY BREAKDOWN AND WENT ABOUT FIXING IT. THE NUMBER-ONE PROBLEM, FOR EXAMPLE, WAS MISSED TACKLES. JUST PRACTICING WASN'T ENOUGH TO FIX IT. THE REASON THEY WERE MISSING SO MANY TACKLES THEN—AND YOU SEE IT TODAY—IS THAT THE DEFENSIVE PLAYERS OFTEN DON'T BRING THEIR BODIES UNDER CONTROL. THEY'RE SO EAGER TO MAKE THE TACKLE, ONE LITTLE HEAD FAKE OR HIP FAKE OR MISSTEP, AND THE GUY IS BY YOU.[39]

— ***Tom Pagna***

The toughest part of my job is recruiting, and the toughest part of recruiting is to convince a boy, especially a boy from a small high school, that he can play here. Ordinary boys seem to feel they can't make it here, but that's a myth.[40]

If I don't have the tenacity, the guts, the willingness to accept the responsibility, under the so-called trying situation that exists, then am I really worthy of the job that I have?[41]

I have never believed in forcing any type of play on the boys. It must be adapted to the personnel. I can't see trying to run with power when I have speed or in trying to use finesse when the players are big and lumbering.[42]

Football can be run a lot of different ways—there's power football, there's finesse football, there's option football, there's the passing game itself with its draws and screens. . . . We were very good at sequencing a base play from which we could pass, screen, draw, reverse, or misdirection—all off that one play.[43]

Generally, people break the chemistry of a football team into four parts—personnel, leadership, strategy, and emotion. Perhaps the ideal situation would be to assign 25 percent to each part. I suppose a fundamentalist such as Vince Lombardi or Sid Gillman puts about an 80-percent emphasis on technique and strategy. For me, the swing would be heavier toward the emotional or psychological factor because I am an emotional coach—I don't deny it.[44]

ARA Q&A

Q: *At Miami of Ohio you played two years under Sid Gillman, who decades later still is remembered as an offensive genius, with many of his innovations still evident in today's game. How do you explain his lasting influence on the game?*

A: Sid was absolutely consumed by football, twenty-four hours a day. He was unbelievable, looking at film all the time, and he was outstanding in developing the passing game. He was the one who brought the passing game to the old All American Conference, which he further developed when he then went to the NFL. That was his strong suit.

Blocking techniques were his thing. Rule blocking is something he brought in to the game. Defenses were so simple then, mostly the 6-2-2-1. If you put a five-man line down instead of a six-man line, no one knew what the heck to do. I remember that happening in high school. We'd practice against the 6-2-2-1, and went out in the championship game in high school, and they gave us a five-man line we hadn't seen before. At halftime, the coach came to me—I was the captain of the team—he said, "All we gotta do . . ." and he's trying to teach the team at halftime how to block a five-man line.

You know how much time you have for that? That was a lesson I learned from that.

Sid Gillman brought rule blocking, and it didn't make one dadgum difference what you lined up in. We had blocking rules. You took the inside gap, that was your first choice, *boom*. Inside gap, over or reach block, and if a man on the inside gap, that's who you took. If there's a man on your nose, you took him. If there was not a man in the gap or over you, then you reached block and hooked him. You follow the rules; just go down the list and do what was called for.

It really accelerated the game. Then defenses brought in a lot of stunting, where they would stack up, say, over a guard, and you get two guys over him to include a backer. Then they had what was "do-dat blocking:" "You do dat and I'll do dat." In other words, the center and the guard have alignment over the guard and the linebacker behind him. So the center is uncovered, but the guard is covered by two guys, one behind the other. The play is going to go to the left. What they would do is the do-dat: the center would reach block, that is put his head in front of the lineman, and the guard would reach-block and go for the linebacker. If the guy over the guard veered

Ara and assistant coach Tom Pagna (left) make a point that a Notre Dame player is apparently taking lying down. University of Notre Dame Archives.

toward the center, that made it an easy block, and the guard could just go and pick up the linebacker. The reverse was true, too—if the guy over the guard would go to his outside, he would be reaching and the center would pick up the blitzing linebacker.

Blocking schemes were at the core of the Gillman philosophy. That was more in college where he developed that, and he was ahead of the field in that respect. When he got into the pros, he became a passing guru. He opened up the attack. Look at old film of both the college and pro games, and they had tighter formations. They used the full-T formation, the full-house backfield, where Gillman came along and got into split ends, flanker backs and motion. He developed a good strategy and he ate up a lot of teams. Then defenses caught up with it, so then it was on to the next level. It's been going on like that for years now.

IV
Ara: His Players

The biggest misconception throughout the country about football players is how academically well they do during the season. They actually maintain higher grades during football season.[1]

THE FUNDAMENTAL DIFFERENCE BETWEEN INTERCOLLEGIATE AND PROFESSIONAL ATHLETES IS THAT IN COLLEGE THE PLAYERS ARE SUPPOSED TO BE STUDENTS FIRST AND FOREMOST. THIS DOES NOT MEAN THAT THEY SHOULD ALL BE PHI BETA KAPPAS OR PHYSICS MAJORS, BUT NEITHER SHOULD THEY BE ABNORMAL STUDENTS MAJORING IN PING-PONG.[2]

— ***Rev. Theodore Hesburgh,***
Notre Dame president, 1952-87

When you coach at a private school, with its high admission requirements, the screening process at the front end almost guarantees that with some counseling and guidance, the youngsters are going to graduate. You're not bringing in the marginal student.[3]

That is the great thing about college athletics. The fact that every four years, at least, there's going to be that turnover. The fact that there are always new challenges. The fact that graduation leaves holes to fill, and, as a result, makes new stars.[4]

Youngsters today are bigger and faster and more skilled when they get here. They have better medical care from birth. They have much better high school coaching than we had twenty, twenty-five years ago. On the other hand, I don't believe today's athlete is as hungry as we were.[5]

We like to get 'em down in weight where their speed is a little greater, where their reaction time is a little quicker, a little sharper.[6]

We may very well be the last bastion of discipline left in the United States. The military doesn't have it the way it used to; schools, churches, and families don't have it. Athletics might be the only thing left where a young man, for two hours or so a day, yields himself to us because he wants to be part of a team.[7]

Some of the old timers might be offended, but they have to understand personnel now. You have 250-pound guys who can run the ball. The difference between skill positions is dramatic.[8]

I live in fear.[9]

— *discussing possible injuries when his team had little depth*

Hope springs eternally, and I was hoping that possibly a super quarterback would turn out. You know, a Joe Theismann or a Terry Hanratty or a John Huarte. But in the quarterback spot it just doesn't happen that way. You become well aware of the fact that they're not exposed to any of the terminology, any of the habits that you teach, any of the formations—and, really, it's a mish-mash as they try to put it all together.[10]

— *referring to freshman players in the few first days of varsity drills*

ARA Q&A

Q: *Millions have seen the movie* Rudy, *the inspirational story of Dan "Rudy" Ruettiger, who walked on to the team while you were there, finally got into a game (1975) and made a late tackle against Georgia Tech before he was carried off the field. What's your take on the Rudy story?*

A: What I remember is that he came to our office. I always had the door open, and my secretary comes in and tells me there is a young man that wanted to walk on to play at Notre Dame. I assumed he was already in school, so I brought him in and chatted with him, and I told him that the first thing we would do is work him out to make sure he wasn't going to hurt himself out there. I had experienced just such a thing and didn't want to have that happen again. Some kids' physical abilities are not up where they think they are.

So I got to talking to him and asked him what courses he was going to pursue, and he told me what he was interested in. Then I asked, "Well, what dorm are you in?" He says, "I'm not in any dorm."

"What do you mean you're not in any dorm?"

"Well, I'm not in school yet. I'm going to go over to Holy Cross Junior College."

"Well, when you get out of Holy Cross Junior College, come and see me."

And he did, got himself eligible and then got onto the field with us and worked his butt off. He was a prep team player and tried like hell. He was just short of some physical ability, height and overall size. Not real fast, either. He came to me in the middle of the 1974 season and said his ambition all his life had been to dress for a home game. I said I had a problem here because the NCAA and university regulations dictate I can only take so many players on the road and can dress only so many at home. But I realized he had earned the right to dress at least once and told him I would do it toward the latter part of the next season. I said, "Next year you will dress for a home game." Things happened and I ended up leaving Notre Dame, and the rest of the story you know from the movie.

One thing the movie fudged on was that he didn't live in the athletic facility, crawling through the window and finding a key left for him. But the basic concept with his determination and overcoming adversity conveyed in that movie are good for young kids.

About Joe Theismann:

Theismann's only weakness is that he doesn't put enough air under the ball—he doesn't have that soft, lob pass. He's only six-foot even but has a strong arm and has a tendency to drill every pass. We're working on it, though.[11]

About John Huarte:

It's like a baseball pitcher who wins only five games one season, then comes up with twenty victories the next. Matter of confidence, probably.[12]

— *discussing Huarte's remarkable turnaround from benchwarmer to 1964 Heisman Trophy winner*

Every time he hits a pass, I think how close we came to not having him around, and I shudder.[13]

Many give us credit for coaching Huarte to become No. 1, but what I did was restore his confidence. I told him he was our quarterback, and even though he might throw five interceptions, he was our man.[14]

To Nick Eddy:

Do you remember what you were doing at this time in 1951? You were seven years old and dreaming of the day when you could play football at Notre Dame. That was the last time Notre Dame beat Purdue in Notre Dame Stadium.[15]

— Parseghian speaking to Eddy before the Irish defeated Purdue at Notre Dame in 1964

They've learned to hold up their heads. They've learned not to say that the other guy is better and give up. They've learned to go out there and play their best, and if they lose, it's not because the other man showed he was better.[16]

— on changing the losing culture at Northwestern

If there is one trait that is common to football coaches, it is that you try to get your best football players in the starting lineup regardless of positions. This sometimes means you'll have a natural fullback playing end or guard, or perhaps an end in the backfield.[17]

We like to get the boys who can run and who may put on some muscle and grow up into a little heavier halfback, rather than the boy who's already big and still has to learn how to run.[18]

It's very easy. I've done it over three hundred times already. And this will prove just how loyal a Notre Dame man you are, because I don't want it to stop you from pushing other boys in the future.[19]

— to a California alumnus offended that Parseghian didn't offer a scholarship to a player endorsed by the alum

There is good football being played in high schools all over the United States. But we try to get the super boy from faraway places and then try to land the solid players in particular areas in the Midwest.[20]

I knew that Notre Dame recruited on a national basis, but it was still a great revelation, seeing it. It is a staggering experience going through all that mail.[21]

We travel as a team.[22]

— referring to a time in 1951 he took his Miami team on the road to Kansas and its hotel wouldn't allow Notre Dame black players to stay

V
Ara: The Motivator

Men, adversity has the effect of eliciting talents that under more prosperous circumstances would have remained dormant.[1]

It's easy to be loyal when you're winning. The real test of attitude is when things turn sour.[2]

Next fall can't some too soon; we have too many scores to settle.[3]

— after winless 1957 season at Northwestern

We must believe—believe in God, believe in ourselves, believe in what we are doing.[4]

Ara confers with quarterback Terry Hanratty during the 1967 Michigan State game. University of Notre Dame Archives.

You can learn to bounce.[5]

— his way of describing the quality to fight another day even though you did not run away the day before

It's not the bounce of the ball that counts, but the bounce of the individual. Every day is not a bright, sunny happening. There are days when it's dark, dismal, and disappointing. There may even be physical or mental anguish troubling you. And the most important thing for an executive, player, or coach to be able to do is to bounce back and meet his next challenge in the eye. You don't quit.[6]

In football, when you get knocked down, what you do next is most important. You get up and carry on. That's what we did. And that's a lesson for all of us. Don't give up.[7]

Each week we go out to win again. Each week is a separate challenge.[8]

No one can buy his way onto a team. You have to earn it. And you do it by dedication and hard work.[9]

Let's not be guilty of not wanting it badly enough![10]

The difference between mediocrity and greatness is a little extra effort.[11]

You just once get flat, you just once relax, and someone will fatten up their reputation at your expense.[12]

The best time to get kids to believe in you is before you need them.[13]

~~~

A good coach will make his players see what they can be rather than what they are.[14]

~~~

Above all I tried to be fair and consistent. Whether a guy was a star player or he was a prep team player, he got the same discipline. Because when you show favoritism, you're really not a leader. And college kids see right through that.[15]

~~~

How . . . can you call yourself a leader when you follow the crowd?[16]

~~~

To be mentally conditioned is to be mentally tough, contact-oriented, with the zeal for the ideal of achieving success.[17]

~~~

May you always be champions where it counts, in your heads![18]

~~~

ARA AND HIS STAFF ARE THE KIND OF PEOPLE YOU HATE TO LET DOWN. IT BREAKS YOUR HEART WHEN YOU DON'T DO WHAT THEY WANT. THEY'RE YOUNG AND ENTHUSIASTIC AND GET CLOSE TO THE GUYS. THEY GET IN THERE AND WORK WITH YOU.[19]

— Jim Carroll, a captain on Ara's first Notre Dame team, in 1964

Dirt! Dirt! That's how Ohio State treats you![20]

—psyching up his Northwestern players in 1958 before they went out and beat the Buckeyes 21-0, a year after Woody Hayes's team had kept the starters in late in a 47-6 victory over Northwestern

YOU CAN'T BE AROUND HIM WITHOUT GETTING ALL WOUND UP YOURSELF.[21]

— Bill Rohr, former Ohio University athletic director and long-time Parseghian friend

Psychologists claim that a person can reach a high point in a ten-game schedule about three times a season. Then it takes ten days to recover. So you try to keep a steady pitch and gradually bring the players up at the week's end.[22]

I was always saying, "No fumbles, no penalties, no mistakes." . . . I didn't believe in wearing them down physically, but sometimes I had to be relentless in what I was trying to get across.[23]

— *preparing his first Notre Dame team, in 1964*

Be men. If an injustice has been done, time will correct it. It'll eventually become a very small thing, but you'll become bigger because of it.[24]

— *to the six players suspended from school for a 1974 dorm incident involving a young woman*

The game is not won by a pep talk on Saturday. It's won by preparation of your club from Monday until game time. If they're not ready on Saturday, then you're not going to get them ready with a dog-eat-dog sermon before the game.[25]

It's just like a thoroughbred in the gate and they won't ring the starter's bell. You let him out a bit, and you bring him back. "Now take it easy, boy. You're going to get out. We're just kind of teasing you a bit." And that's exactly what happens here. They get all enthused, and the mental aspect builds up because they're not working as hard physically.[26]

— *on how he prepped his players for a game by building them up and then tapering off*

Progress is our most important product.[27]

— *one of several signs he had posted at Northwestern*

Ҩ

We will rise from these ashes.[28]

— *after Notre Dame's 40-6 loss to Nebraska in 1973 Orange Bowl*

Ҩ

You learn early in athletics that you'll have ups and downs. You are going to get knocked down, but you don't lie there. You get up and face the challenge.[29]

Ҩ

Everything worthwhile must be bought with sacrifice.[30]

Ҩ

Always a second chance, sometimes a third, but never more than that.[31]

Ҩ

When you wake up in the morning ask yourself,
How can I better myself today?
And when you go to bed ask yourself,
How did I better myself today?
And if you can think of one thing,
Then you have bettered yourself.[32]

Ҩ

Ara was a pretty decent running back at Miami (Ohio) University, good enough in fact to play some in the NFL with the Cleveland Browns. University of Notre Dame Archives.

Success won't happen by sitting here. We've got to keep on striving.[33]

Every man can be successful in life, regardless of his personal endowments or the lack of them. What matters only is that the man must be hungry, he must have an all-consuming desire to succeed.[34]

I demand complete dedication from myself, my coaches, and my team. The only road to success in football is hard work and more hard work. I don't mean that the game can't be fun, but there's no exception to the hard work rule for a winning team.[35]

We used to tell our teams that they should have no breaking point, that they should play so hard that the other team broke first.[36]

When I make a fist, it's strong and you can't tear it apart. As long as there's unity, there's strength.[37]

Look at any famous upset in college football, and you'll find one constant factor—the overwhelming desire to win. Scouting, surprise plays, "breaks," fumbles, penalties, bad weather all enter into the upset picture, of course, but most coaches agree that wanting to win is the real key.[38]

We win because winning isn't everything.[39]

MR. PARSEGHIAN IS A LITTLE BIT NAPOLEONIC, BUT HE SURE KNOWS WHAT YOU HAVE TO DO TO WIN.[40]

— ***unnamed protege of Parseghian's***

I didn't work by the hour, I worked by the job, by what had to be done. I didn't consider it work.[41]

VI
Ara: Polls, Bowls, and Big Games

Opening games in my first year or in fifty years will always be the same. It's the most important game on the schedule. The first game sets the pace, the tempo, for the season.[1]

I prefer to think of it as a 9-½-½ record.[2]

— *referring to the 1964 season that ended 9-1 with a loss in the last two minutes at Southern Cal*

(NOTRE DAME) WAS INVINCIBLE UNTIL THE LAST NINETY-FIVE SECONDS OF THE SEASON IN PLAYING ONE OF THE MOST CHALLENGING INTERSECTIONAL SCHEDULES OF THE YEAR AND PARTICULARLY IN CONSIDERATION OF THE FACT THAT IT SUCCEEDED FAR BEYOND WHAT WAS EXPECTED.[3]

— Vince Draddy, chairman of the National Football Foundation, upon rewarding Notre Dame in 1964 with the MacArthur Bowl, which supports the argument that Parseghian actually won three national titles at Notre Dame, not just the two consensus titles his teams won in 1966 and 1973

THE 10-10 TIE

We were going into the wind, and they had a great field goal kicker. We punched out a first down, but with the clock running out, and all the elements against us, we ran out the clock.[4]

We'd fought hard to come back and tie it up. After all that, I didn't want to risk giving it to them cheap.[5]

THE 10-10 TIE (CONT.)

To critics claiming he was content to play for a tie

My rebuttal to those people today is, "You tell me what happened. How'd we go for a tie?" They really don't know. There was an impression created, and the impression prevailed.[6]

The game had such a build-up that everyone wanted a conclusion. The fact that we used conservative plays at the end made me the bad guy. Everybody wanted me to throw the bomb. That's what it boils down to. They wanted to coach my team.[7]

That was one of the most beautiful football games that has ever been played.[8]

If you take all those circumstances and put them into a computer, I'd like to see what comes out. I made the decision on percentages.[9]

— explaining why he played ball control on Notre Dame's final possession late in the Michigan State game, with the wind at MSU's back, the Spartans had a strong field-goal kicker, and four of the Irish's top offensive players, including quarterback Terry Hanratty and running back Nick Eddy, were on the bench injured

Since 1966 there have been a number of guys who have gone for the tie. But everyone still remembers me.[10]

OLD NOTRE DAME WILL TIE OVER ALL. SING IT OUT, GUYS. THAT IS NOT EXACTLY WHAT THE MARCH SAYS, OF COURSE, BUT THAT IS HOW THE BIG GAME ENDS EVERY TIME YOU REPLAY IT.[11]

***— Dan Jenkins, writing his lead to the 10-10 tie in* Sports Illustrated**

Tying is bad, but there's something worse. That's losing. We still had Southern Cal the next week. We get a chance to get back to No. 1 alone by beating Southern Cal. If we gamble and lose to Michigan State, the next week we're fighting for No. 2 and maybe No. 10 in the rankings.[12]

There was only one way we could lose our chance to win the national championship, and that was by losing that game. Michigan State's season would be over, and we still had one game left to play.[13]

I vowed to bring a national championship to the student body some day. I didn't know how or when, but I vowed we would do it.[14]

— referring to Notre Dame's No. 1 spot in both the AP and UPI polls after the Irish ended their 9-0-1 season in 1966 with a 51-0 victory over Southern Cal

Time will vindicate us.[15]

ARA Q&A

Q: *Notre Dame won two national titles under Parseghian—in 1966 after a 9-0-1 season and in 1973, when the Irish finished 11-0 with a 24-23 Sugar Bowl victory over Alabama. Another school of thought says that Parseghian actually won three national titles, also taking into account that in Ara's first season, 1964, Notre Dame was awarded the MacArthur Bowl, presented by the National Football Foundation and symbolic of college football supremacy. The Irish were named winners of the prestigious award in light of their 9-0 start, although they would end their season a week later with a controversial 20-17 loss at Southern Cal that featured what Parseghian described as questionable officiating on several key occasions. Alabama, which finished 11-0, was voted No. 1 in the final Associated Press and United Press International polls. So, Ara, do you believe you won two or three national titles at Notre Dame?*

A: We've only officially claimed two, but the thing about it—and John Gaski (a Notre Dame marketing professor) recently has made a big issue of this. He points out that we should claim a third national championship because we were named the national champions before the Southern Cal game in 1964.

There have been other similar circumstances in which a team has been awarded a national title before a late loss. Consider the 1973 Alabama team; it had the same benefit when they won one national championship (UPI) before we played them and beat them in the Sugar Bowl.

Gaski has written a number of letters promoting the notion that we did in fact win a national title in 1964. The most recent letter he wrote was in May 2009 to Athletic Director Jack Swarbrick in which he addressed this issue with all the rationales, pleading for the school to officially recognize 1964 as a championship season. He did the same thing a few years ago with former athletic director Kevin White. It was three or four pages long.

While others have been taking issue with it, I personally am not petitioning it nor pursuing it. I'm just irritated because of the Alabama situation. If they get to claim that, then we should take the 1964 team and accept the national championship. That's what the MacArthur Bowl is all about—and I have it hanging right here on my wall.

Editor's note: While Alabama won both polls in 1964 and finished 10-1, Arkansas, 11-0, also staked a claim when it was picked No. 1 by several rating systems. Notre Dame had two other Parseghian-led seasons in which the Irish got some No. 1 mention: 1967 and 1970.

We were novices, obviously, in the bowl business. . . . We had to figure out the number of players who would be going, what staff members should go, whether the families could go, when to leave for Dallas, all of it had to be figured.[16]

— on Notre Dame's trip to 1970 Cotton Bowl to play Texas, ending 44-year moratorium on bowl games

I've had some exciting moments in twenty-one years of coaching, but in view of Texas's credentials, I'd have to say this was the biggest. We broke their thirty-game winning streak, we held the nation's top rushing team more than 150 yards below their average; we held the nation's top scoring team to only one touchdown.[17]

— on the 24-11 victory over No. 1 Texas in the 1971 Cotton Bowl

Basically, what we tried to do was mirror their wishbone. We wanted to force Texas into a passing situation, to make them come out of their full-house backfield.[18]

— referring to Cotton Bowl victory over Texas in 1971

After the 1970 season, in which Notre Dame (10-1) beat No. 1 Texas in the Cotton Bowl, and Nebraska (11-0-1) defeated LSU in the Orange Bowl, there was some debate over No. 1:

Nebraska Coach Bob Devaney: I can't see how the Pope himself could vote for Notre Dame.

Ara Parseghian: I thought the remark about the Pope wasn't in the best of taste.[19]

— Nebraska won the AP poll and finished with 39 first-place votes to Notre Dame's eight.

I'll tell you one thing, we didn't hide our heads in the sand. We met the competition.[20]

— referring to the 1972 season, when the Irish agreed to play a powerful Nebraska team in the Orange Bowl, while Alabama's Bear Bryant took his undefeated team to the Cotton Bowl to play lower-ranked Texas

The 1973 team is real special. I had never coached against Bear Bryant. Alabama had never played Notre Dame. It was North against the South; the Catholics against the Baptists. Both teams were undefeated, and everything on the line.[21]

— referring to his only unbeaten, untied team

We wanted to maintain possession, but there was no chance we were going to make it by running. If (Robin) Weber wasn't open, then we'd wind up punting, and the only risk was Tom (Clements) slipping in the end zone. There has been more acknowledgment of that play than was due it, and there has been more criticism than deserved for our (1966) Michigan State game.[22]

— referring to the third-down pass out of the end zone that sealed a 24-23 win over Alabama in the 1973 Sugar Bowl

I didn't overburden the team with this being my last game. I thanked them as profoundly as I could after the game.[23]

— after Notre Dame's 13-11 victory over Alabama in 1975 Orange Bowl

We have beaten Alabama twice and Texas once, each time they were unbeaten and ranked No. 1. We haven't dodged anyone. We played a great Nebraska team with one of our lesser teams, and that probably was a mistake. But we have taken them all on.[24]

Taking nothing away from Alabama, there was a recent year when their longest trip was to Knoxville, Tennessee. Every year Notre Dame plays from coast to coast, and we go as far south as Miami. There should be some system of putting all of the factors, won-lost records, conference strength, difficulty of schedule, and others into a computer and coming up with a realistic national rating.[25]

I've pushed for a national playdown at the end of the year. It's up to the NCAA to do something about it. They should study the situation. A playoff is the only way to really determine an overall champion.[26]

It comes up every year around the end of the season, when the bowl games are hot, then it dies out when everyone starts thinking about basketball. What we need is to hire somebody on a fulltime basis to pursue the problems of putting together playoffs.[27]

The likelihood of an extended playoff to determine the national champion is extremely remote.[28]

We're scheduling ten years in advance. How can you predict who's going to be that good that far ahead? It all runs in cycles. If you're around twenty-five years the way I have been, you can see that.[29]

A bowl game is an ideal supplement for a team's unpredictable schedule. I use the word 'unpredictable' instead of 'inadequate.' With football schedules being arranged many years in advance, you cannot accurately predict the strength of the opponents you will face.[30]

— making the case for a Challenge Bowl that would match the top two teams after the bowls

The polls are great. They give you the relative strength of the teams around the country. We all recognize that on any given Saturday, anything can happen. No. 1 can lose to No. 19—it's part of the game. But it doesn't mean polls are not inaccurate.[31]

We have not won as many late-season games as we'd like. But I'd rather birdie the first hole than double-bogey it. Being an independent, we drop right out of the polls if we lose early in the year.[32]

Ara hoists the Sugar Bowl trophy after the Irish downed Alabama, 24-23, in the 1973 Sugar Bowl game to complete a perfect 11-0 season and wrap up a national title. University of Notre Dame Archives.

ARA Q&A

Q: *In recent years major college football officials have talked about tweaking the Bowl Championship Series (BCS) to make it a BCS Plus One format in which the top two teams after the bowl games would play each other in one last grand finale game to determine a national champion. This proposal has been hailed as a modern-day innovation to end the controversy of picking a true national champion without a playoff. If the BCS Plus One deal sounds like a revelation, it shouldn't. Parseghian, somewhat of a maverick in his day, called for such a post-bowl,*

winner-take-all game more than thirty years ago, long before there was a BCS. He called his idea "the Challenge Bowl." What was your thinking, Ara?

A: I've always been for having a national championship playoff, and I tried like hell without success to get one. All the evidence you need is this constant bickering about this mythical championship. Voting for it certainly was not an adequate way to do it.

I'd go through this every year. I'd go to the American Football Coaches Association meeting, and that would be the topic, "We've got to do something." We would come up with these various ideas, but the bowl system was very firm—they didn't want anyone tinkering with it. After I got out of coaching, they were able to get the Bowl Championship Series going, and that was a step in the right direction. Even with that, though, you still have these arguments about who really deserves it. There is no perfect scenario. I was a great supporter of a national playoff.

My idea of a Challenge Bowl? Reaction was mixed. If you were talking to someone in the Big Ten, which had a long-term contract with the Rose Bowl, they looked down their noses at it. They wanted to hold on to what they had. But if you talked to some school that came out of a small conference with a perfect record, boy, they wanted a piece of that right now. It was like spinning your wheels. Of course, I was a coach and not an athletic director, and next thing I know each year after the convention is that I had to get back to recruiting responsibilities and everything else that goes along with coaching. Talk of change would fade out, nothing happened, and the cycle would start all over again the next year.

We didn't put Oklahoma on probation, the NCAA did. We made the decision to try and discourage teams from breaking the rules and to try and bring some sanity to this business of recruiting. You can't go out and eulogize a man who's in jail and make him man of the year. It wasn't aimed just at Oklahoma. It was aimed at everybody who breaks the rules.[33]

— explaining the final 1974 UPI coaches' poll, which didn't include Oklahoma, which had finished 11-0 but was on NCAA probation. Southern Cal finished No. 1 in the UPI poll, while Oklahoma topped the AP's final poll.

ARA Q&A

Q: *Of the ninety-five games your Notre Dame teams won, or ninety-six if you include the 10-10 tie with Michigan State, which was the closest to a perfect game that one of your teams played?*

A: To consider that, you have to start with the importance of the game, the significance. Picking one is near impossible. There's the 1973 Southern Cal game at home, which we won, 23-14, where we were very consistent and played a good game on both sides of the ball. So many factors go into it. Like, did you play a perfect game when you beat Navy, 48-0? No, because the opposition wasn't as strong. You need to take into account what happened the year before, how the rankings will be influenced by the result, and what it means to how the bowl picture will be affected.

There's the Michigan State-Notre Dame game in 1966 (which ended in a 10-10 tie). The buildup to that game was unbelievable. There was so much riding on the outcome of that game. I don't remember ever thinking after any game that we had just played the perfect game. Some might say our 24-11 win over No. 1 Texas in the 1971 Cotton Bowl.

When I look at that game, I see an opponent that turned the ball over to us a bunch of times. The key to that game for us was how we defensed Texas fullback Steve Worster. We would false step the guy. Our outside backer would step to the outside like he was going to go after the pitch, then he would push off with that foot. The quarterback would be reading our guy, thinking he was going upfield, only for the backer to push off that outside foot and cut straight to the fullback area, and we were able to cause several fumbles because of that. It's a technique we used because of their triple option, and their first option was to give the fullback the ball. If you stop that, the quarterback keeps it, and if you stop that, the quarterback pitches it out. Everything is an action and a counteraction. That's when we used a mirror defense on them.

But it's almost impossible to play a perfect game. Such a game would imply no penalties, no turnovers, perfect blocking, and perfect tackling, and that just doesn't happen.

Our problem is that we did not have a good week of preparation. It was twenty to thirty degrees all week. The cold weather seems to thicken the blood or something.[34]

— following the 55-24 loss in Los Angeles to Southern Cal in 1974, after the Irish had led 24-0 late in the first half

VII
Ara: With Feeling

We already accept that the interest and adrenaline, the tears and the grief, are not just restricted to the players.[1]

Emotions are powerful. Yet while they build a drive which temporarily equalizes otherwise unequal individuals or teams, they also lead to letdowns after a major game. The successful coach is the one who best controls this letdown factor.[2]

What we do here and now will follow us for many years . . . to cry foul, to alibi, would undo much that this season has done. If you've got to scream, if you want to cry, swear, or punch a locker, do it now. . . . But after we open the doors, I want all of you to hold your tongues.[3]

— to his players after the heartbreaking 20-17 loss in the last two minutes at Southern Cal to end the 1964 season, Ara's first at Notre Dame, 9-1

Adulation and adversity are the main emotions in life. You experience these emotions in football as well as the classroom. There is a place for college football for the complete education of a young man, and I don't think college football has stepped out of its boundaries.[4]

I make no bones about it. I shed tears.[5]

— referring to the suspension of six players for summer 1974 dorm incident involving young female acquaintance

I pleaded their case before the administration. I could see the immense remorsefulness they experienced through three weeks of not knowing what would happen to them. That, in itself, was a terrible penalty.[6]

I just got back to campus, and one of the secretaries here rushed up to congratulate me. So I gave her a hug and hit her over the head with the trophy. Thank God she wasn't hurt.[7]

— after the 1973 Sugar Bowl win over Alabama

At Northwestern, no one knew who I was. But it got to be difficult, kids asking for autographs. I always obliged. I always thought about how I would feel as a kid. But it got so I relished the opportunity to go home and have a dinner with my wife, put my feet up by the fireplace and relax. Those were the great moments of the year.[8]

I've been in a lot of locker rooms in my twenty-one years of coaching. But the jubilation of our team today was something I haven't experienced in a long time.[9]

— after victory over No. 1 Texas in 1971 Cotton Bowl

I'm a terrible loser. That's one of my worst qualities. I feel totally responsible for losing. I know I didn't do something right.[10]

Even after twenty-eight years, I feel a little bit like the guy who lost his best girlfriend. I was loyal to Northwestern. I busted my tail, and all of a sudden they don't want me? You feel rejected.[11]

— recalling the lack of a vote of confidence from Northwestern Athletic Director Stu Holcomb after the Wildcats finished 5-4 in 1963, a year after being 6-0 at one point and ranked No. 1

Actor Sean Astin (left), who starred in the movie Rudy, *is joined by the real Dan "Rudy" Ruettiger (middle) and Ara at a movie premiere event in 1993.* University of Notre Dame Archives.

I don't want to spoil the game for you. I'm going home.[12]

— *leaving a radio booth at Notre Dame's first home game after his resignation, after spending much of the first half fidgeting and fussing*

THE LOSS TO PURDUE EARLY IN THE SEASON HIT HIM HARDER THAN ANY LOSS I HAD SEEN THROUGH THE YEARS. THE MOMENTS OF LEVITY AND GOOD HUMOR WERE FEWER AND FARTHER APART. HE LOOKED DREADFUL. HE HAD CREVICES IN HIS FACE THAT LOOKED LIKE THE GRAND CANYON.[13]

— ***Katie Parseghian, after 31-20 Purdue loss in 1974***

NIEMANN-PICK TYPE C DISEASE

That thought of kids losing their mind—I don't know ... It's got to be one of the cruelest diseases on the planet for kids. And for parents, if they can't remember who you are.[14]

— in 1993, after three of his grandchildren were diagnosed with the disease, Ara helped form the Ara Parseghian Medical Research Foundation.His daughter-in-law Cindy Parseghian is president of the foundation. The three grandchildren eventually died from the disease.

I don't think any parents should outlive their children, or that any grandparents should outlive their grandchildren.[15]

Medical research is a grinding process. It's expensive, it's ongoing, and you go in little bits. You'd like them to get the silver bullet right now.[16]

We have a goal. You immerse yourself in that.[17]

— speaking of finding a cure

I was at the time of my life when you think you're on the senior citizen side and there may be some retirement and recreational activities that you've worked all your life for, and all of a sudden it changes your life completely. There was a period where I was just stunned.[18]

I've always been optimistic; I've always felt that if there were a challenge, it could be won. We've had sayings, and I used them with the team; we have no breaking point, there's no circumstances we can't overcome. I believe it in my heart.[19]

VIII
Ara: Keeping It Real

I learned one thing long ago, though, never argue with an opinion. I give the facts, and let it go with that.[1]

— *speaking to Notre Dame cynics convinced that the football program cheated to be so successful*

If I go and buy an athlete, what am I telling him then from my position of authority? I've taught him the worst kind of lesson I can right from the beginning: a superior convincing him that cheating is okay to do.[2]

Let's put the thing in proper perspective. If even a hint of that was present, why would they play so well in the first half? There was absolutely zero activity at halftime as far as any racial problems were concerned. It was an elated halftime, because we were kickin' their (butt).[3]

— addressing a newspaper report that claims there was halftime dissension and a decision by some Notre Dame players to purposely not try in the second half of the 1974 loss at Southern Cal, 55-24, a game in which Notre Dame led 24-6 at the half

On Gerry Faust:

He's a terrific guy. He bubbles with enthusiasm. A man of integrity. Religious. You gotta love him. But you gotta say to yourself, knowing what I know, "Hey, Gerry. Pace yourself."[4]

God doesn't favor one team over another—this is a game to be played.[5]

I'm embarrassed by this stuff about being a legend. I got a letter once from a priest who said he liked me because I was a simple and friendly man. Because I was a simple guy. Thank God, he didn't say simple-minded, but I consider that letter one of the great compliments I've gotten.[6]

We had to explain ourselves a couple times (to the NCAA) when I was at Notre Dame, but it wasn't for felonies. To me, the felonies are doctoring transcripts, not insisting a kid go to school when he comes, and buying the athlete.[7]

"Everybody does it." That's one of the worst copouts of the guys who are apprehended. "Everybody does it." Bull! The guy who's been caught says that because it's the rationalization that lets him say, "I went ahead and compromised the rules because I had to face the kind of competition that was doing it."[8]

— referring to Southern Methodist University, which became the first school assessed the NCAA's death penalty

We only have to look at what has happened in Washington (D.C.) the last few years to understand some of the things that go on in recruiting. The men in Washington are supposed to be our leaders . . . If you understand Watergate, then you understand many of the recruiting violations.[9]

The success-failure syndrome in football is greater. Your mistakes are reviewed, analyzed, and dissected by millions of people. Believe me, that is pressure.[10]

~

I never got any pressure from the administration. But I found myself defending a team for going 9-2 (in 1974). We went 11-0 and won the national championship last year (1973). When you're 11-0 as a coach the only thing you can do is duplicate it. You can't improve on it, but you can get . . . worse.[11]

~

A baseball manager has 154 games to operate in. He can lose in April or May and still come out on top. But in football you have only nine games. Every Saturday is do-or-die.[12]

— *spoken in 1957, between his first and second seasons at Northwestern, and several years before Major League Baseball expanded to a 162-game schedule*

~

On Monday, the student paper at Northwestern ripped me up for being happy that we won by a revolting score like 7-6.[13]

— *referring to a victory over Notre Dame in 1960, when Notre Dame's Joe Perkowski missed an extra point*

~

I learned a long time ago that it doesn't matter whether you win by one point or forty, when the season is over it goes on your record as a win.[14]

Be men. If an injustice has been done, time will correct it. It'll eventually become a very small thing, but you'll become bigger because of it.[15]

IX
Ara: His Humor

This is what we're up against. In the 1966 Sugar Bowl, Alabama was beating Nebraska so bad at halftime, Coach (Bear) Bryant didn't even go into the locker room to talk to his team. He went to a concession stand, bought two bags of potato chips, and a carton of Pepsi, and fed all eighty thousand people at the game.[1]

— *at high school football banquet before 1973 Sugar Bowl, in which Notre Dame was to play, and defeat, Alabama*

I was play-boxing with Mike, and that little stinker got a punch in.[2]

— *referring to gash over his eye put there by his son Mike*

I know all about those charts. They say I'm supposed to weigh 175. Can you imagine how I'd look at 175? Like death warmed over.[3]

Where's my wife? I've got to find her. I want to congratulate her for marrying me.[4]

— after 1973 victory over Miami gave Notre Dame its first perfect season under Parseghian

I am in a position to tell you now that Father (Edmund) Joyce didn't like one of my pet ideas. I suggested that it would be appropriate if, instead of a shamrock mounted on the Irish helmet, we had a camel wandering across the desert.[5]

— joking about why he walked out before a press conference to announce his hiring as Notre Dame coach

When you're a retired coach, you have the tendency to be eulogized often.[6]

Can you imagine me eating a hot dog before a game?[7]

— eating a press box foot-long before the 1975 Missouri-Alabama game, his first as a color commentator for ABC

Got an anonymous letter advising me that the field telephone between me and my spotters would be tapped on Saturday. Probably a crank.[8]

— *from a diary entry he wrote for* Life *magazine the week of the 1959 Northwestern-Notre Dame game, won 30-24 by Parseghian's Wildcats*

I'm a genius. Another one of those beautifully designed plays.[9]

— *describing the late-game Tom Clements pass from the end zone in the 1973 Sugar Bowl to reserve tight end Robin Weber, who was supposed to be a decoy on the play*

One fan told me, "We're with you, Ara, win or tie." You notice he didn't say anything about losing.[10]

The Cotton Bowl didn't have synthetic turf then (1970), and the field was really saturated during the week leading up to the game. Helicopters were brought in to beat down the field, and I can remember (Texas coach) Darrell Royal's comment. He said, "Well, we've got a million-dollar game and a ten-cent field."[11]

We're glad to have Dwight Chapin of the *Los Angeles Times* with us today, and we thank Judge Sirica for allowing him to be here.[12]

— making a play on names at a 1974 press conference, referring to the "other" Dwight Chapin involved in the Watergate trial

It looks like a couple of presidential candidates are here. . . . Want to talk about Vietnam?[13]

— at a joint press conference with Texas Coach Darrell Royal prior to the 1971 Cotton Bowl, after looking out and seeing the sea of media facing them

I'll never forget the decision (we) made years ago, and that's that we go out at least two nights a week. She goes out on Mondays, and I go out on Wednesdays.[14]

— joking to player Jim Seymour when asked the secret to his marriage to Katie

"Erin O'Parseghian."

— joking about how he refers to himself when speaking to Irish groups

"Angelino Parmeghan."[15]

— for Italian audiences

All kidding aside, a pair of legendary coaches meet on the field prior to the 1973 Sugar Bowl—Alabama's Paul "Bear" Bryant and Ara. University of Notre Dame Archives.

I must confess; I worked with the defense last week.[16]

— at Monday Notre Dame Quarterback Club luncheon two days after 8-7 victory over Purdue in 1971

I had a number of opportunities to go (coach in the NFL), but I didn't go. Right now I think I would, considering the salaries they're paying. As a matter of fact, if they called me right now (2005), sure I'll go! One year![17]

The game was in South Bend, but it could just as well have been deep in the heart of Dixie. There were three Big Ten officials and two from the Southwest Conference. I knew we were in trouble when one of the Southwest guys grunted, "The Yankees win the toss."[18]

— *referring to a 1974 home game against Rice*

Spoke at a luncheon and there were questions. "Have you planned any special plays for the Rose Bowl game?" Ha, ha, very funny. All I have to do is play Notre Dame next and they've got us in the Rose Bowl already.[19]

— *from a diary he wrote for* Life *magazine the week of the 1959 Northwestern-Notre Dame game, won 30-24 by Parseghian's Wildcats*

Gentlemen, have you blessed your coach today?[20]

— *upon running into a dozen of his Notre Dame players coming out of church after early Mass*

HEY, ARA, RUN OUT AND GET US A CUP OF COFFEE.[21]

— Woody Hayes, when Ara was a freshman coach at Miami (Ohio) University

Two weeks ago after Navy (a comeback 14-6 Notre Dame victory), I told the team they were definitely causing my hair to turn gray. Today I told them they were going to make me a replacement for Kojak.[22]

— following a late 14-10 victory over Pittsburgh referring to the bald TV detective played by Telly Savalas

X
Ara: His Resignation

On the plane back from the (1974) Navy game was when I made my decision. The post-game exhaustion after that game was incredible.[1]

~~~

Nobody knew except my wife, my brother Jerry, and Father Joyce and Father Hesburgh. Then, in December, Dan Devine released the story to a Minnesota writer. I was irritated by that; it was very unfair.[2]

~~~

I can count on one hand the number of coaches who have bowed out gracefully. Most are fired, retire, or die. I resigned. That was a difficult thing.[3]

~~~
~~~

Those were very true pictures that were taken. I was drawn, my eyes were sunk back in my head. Twenty-five years of coaching caught up to me. The long hours—I've always been an early riser. The pressure of the season—I worked myself and my staff maybe too hard. I've looked back and asked myself why it was that way, and realized I wouldn't have had the success I did without doing it that way. You have to operate in a manner based on your own personality, on your own makeup. I didn't change over the years. I remained excitable. I always got emotionally involved.[4]

I can see it; I've become less patient, more irritable, and physically and emotionally drained.[5]

AS FAR AS I'M CONCERNED, ARA CAN TAKE OFF COACHING FOREVER.[6]

— ***Katie Parseghian, Ara's wife***

She doesn't have much drag in this family.[7]

— *Ara's response, with a smile*

My wife was fearful I would change my mind after USC (55-24 loss). But I had made a rational decision for rational reasons. So I resigned.[8]

I'm totally convinced that if I hadn't given up the game when I did, I'd either be on the funny farm or six feet under.[9]

Moose (Krause) came to my house and said, "Ara, I'll resign if you take the job as athletic director." To me that was unbelievable. He was willing to make that sacrifice on my behalf.[10]

I found the pace of life I was going at to be a more sane pace. Also, shortly after I stepped aside, over a period of three years, I had five major surgeries. I had a kidney stone removed, my gall bladder removed—I was deathly sick with both of those. I had arthroscopic knee surgery. I had two hip replacements. So some self-doubts set in as to whether or not I was physically capable of returning to the game.[11]

Frank Leahy was there eleven years. I lasted eleven years. Lou Holtz lasted eleven years. I think there's a time when the self-imposed pressure to continue to be at the very top level—the level where there's no margin of error—gets to you. You've got to win every game, and every time you look across the field, there's a team that wants to make its reputation by beating you. I can attest to that because I stood on that other sideline.[12]

Pre-game moments were agony. And Saturday mornings were difficult. It was all self-inflicted pressure. There just didn't seem to be any margin for error. I was blaming myself for every little thing; if the buses were late or the hotel reservations weren't in order.[13]

I was on a treadmill, and I couldn't seem to get off.[14]

No way I'm going to sit on my duff the entire season. I'm waiting until the middle of December or early January to see if I really miss coaching. If I get itchy feet, then I'll get back into it.[15]

— *spoken about a year after his 1974 resignation*

Ara on the sidelines for 1973 Air Force game en route to national title, although the stress was showing even during this 48-15 blowout. University of Notre Dame Archives.

I've always said twenty-five years of coaching college football was enough for me. Although I've learned in my life never to say "never," I don't seriously think I will ever coach again.[16]

— *in 1982 amid rumors he was going to the NFL to coach*

I have an abundance of things to accomplish, and I'll go after them as long as the challenge remains. Happiness is what life is all about, and if I wasn't now finding my life fulfilled, I'd already be back in coaching.[17]

— *announcing in 1978 he wasn't returning to coaching*

It was if I had willed myself to keep going until I couldn't coach anymore. I've watched myself in the (documentary) movie about Notre Dame football called *Wake Up the Echoes*. In the beginning, I have coal black hair. In the end, I'm gray with all these wrinkles. I look better now than I did when I was coaching.[18]

— spoken several years after he turned sixty

I feel very good healthwise. I was living at much too fast a pace during my eleven years at Notre Dame. I'm in excellent health right now. My blood pressure is normal, with control. I don't have the anxiety I had during the last year of my coaching career.[19]

— speaking in December 1975, a year after resigning from Notre Dame and while also announcing he wouldn't be returning to coaching in 1976

ARA Q&A

Q: *In the years after you stepped down as Notre Dame coach, there were many times your name was linked to one National Football League job or another. How close did you ever come to taking an NFL job?*

A: Not really close after leaving Notre Dame. When I was at Northwestern, though, I got a call one Monday for the Minnesota Vikings job. This would have been about 1960. I flew up to Minnesota, and the general manager picks me up at the airport, and we drive straight to the stadium. I had taken a flight early in the morning, and it's a short flight. When we got to the stadium, we went straight to the VIP lounge, stocked with liquor, and he starts drinking. He says, "Do you want a drink?" and I said, "Not at 10:30 in the morning." He looked like he was sloshing them down pretty good. I then had an interview, and it was a positive one, but I thought to myself, 'I don't think I want to come up here and work for this guy. He's in the bag, and it's still morning.'

I also had a number of opportunities when I was at Notre Dame. Edward Bennett Williams, the lawyer, wanted to hire me with the Washington Redskins (Williams was team president). He calls me with the kind of offer you don't want to turn down. He tells me, "Look, I'm coming up there to see you." That's how badly he wanted to talk about it. I said, "Don't come. I'm a college football coach, and I don't have an interest." He says, "No, I'm coming up there."

So he comes up there to Notre Dame. This had to be around 1967, because we still had our offices in the Rock, and the ACC (Athletic and Convocation Center) hadn't been built. Anyway, he comes into my office with a briefcase and opens it up. I said, "You know, I told you this would be a wasted trip. I'm sorry." He lays out this whole business plan. But I wasn't leaving.

Joe Robbie did the same thing for me with the Miami Dolphins: "You'll have a limousine driver, you're going to have a house, you're going to have a long-term contract." Those were the kinds of things he said to me, but a couple things influenced me not to take any of these offers. One, I liked being around the university atmosphere in a university town. Also, I didn't want to move my children into a big city—they were growing and they were comfortable here. Those were the two factors that kept me in college football.

XI
Ara: This and That

BALANCE

In the modern era, running up win streaks is difficult. This is unusual because of the balance there is in college football. The population explosion has given, in my opinion, better facilities, and coaching techniques has produced outstanding talent for a lot of teams.[1]

GOLF

I'm an absolute golf nut. I pursue golf the same way as I do anything else. I have to find a way to lick that nutty game.[2]

MEDIA

Give the TV people an inch now, and they try to own your life. It's why we had to make Terry Hanratty out of bounds to anybody. Gosh, I mean, the kid has got to go to school.[3]

MICHIGAN

I remember when we were talking about getting that series going, thinking it was unlikely that I'd ever get to coach in one of those. I mean, how long can you coach at Notre Dame?[4]

— referring to 1967 talks between Notre Dame and Michigan that led to scheduling each other, but not starting until 1978—four years after Parseghian's resignation

NORTHWESTERN

I don't know whether the Irish are within a step or a foot or even an inch of being a real, good team. But they're close. An eight-cylinder engine, with tremendous horsepower, will sputter and drag if you take out a couple of sparkplugs or don't have them put in.[5]

— after Parseghian's Northwestern team annihilated the Irish 35-6 in 1962, one of four straight times Ara and the Wildcats defeated Notre Dame

OHIO STATE

I'm disappointed we haven't been able to play them. I think possibly if the news media would talk it up a little bit more, maybe down the line we could get a game.[6]

— expressing his desire to play the Buckeyes, although Ohio State Coach Woody Hayes said he didn't want to play Notre Dame

O. J. SIMPSON

I believe he ran thirty-eight times against us, and he really was hit hard on a few occasions. Each time I'd say to myself, That will slow him down. But a couple of plays later, he'd be away for a touchdown.[7]

OPPORTUNITY

If the idea of a routine nine-to-five job turns you off, I want to tell you about a fascinating new career opportunity.[8]

— *comments attributed to Parseghian in an ad that featured him endorsing Florida-based Deltona, a community builder and developer*

POLITICS

Our confidence in politicians today is less than what we'd like to be, and as a result anything that comes out as a positive statement is open to speculation. I've seen it happen. A guy says something one week, and the next week he does something else.[9]

PRAYER

We pray before and after every game. I think religion is a very important thing.[10]

Know we're all not of the same religious persuasion. I think the Lord's prayer ought to cover everyone.[11]

— to his first Miami freshman team before its first game

PRIVACY

THE MOST AGGRAVATING CALLS ARE THE ONES FROM THE WEST COAST—PERSONS WHO FORGET THE TIME DIFFERENCE AND PHONE IN THE MIDDLE OF THE NIGHT.[12]

— Katie Parseghian

SOCIETY

I think we're in a better cycle all around on campus right now. We're out of the hippie movement, the flower children, the drug aspects pretty much, I believe, and a very unpopular war has ended. In my opinion, the Vietnam war was a far greater contributor to campus rebellion than we realized.[13]

SPORTSMANSHIP

No one hates seeing a player hurt more than I. It is the stinking part of the game no one can control. But whatever you feel, play clean. The worst thing you can do to any team is beat them.[14]

STEWARDSHIP

You know what that was? That was word that Howard Cosell just donated $10,000 to the National Multiple Sclerosis Foundation. Imagine this! I'm the national chairman, you know, and I just talked to Howard about it once, a few weeks ago. Now he's giving us $10,000. How do you like that?[15]

— on taking phone call during an interview with reporter

TOUCHDOWN JESUS

Certainly it's wonderful to have the "Touchdown Jesus" mural towering over the field as part of the Notre Dame tradition. But that image can't block or tackle.[16]

UNPREDICTABILITY

You'd be amazed at the number of things that can happen when you have a seventy-five-man squad. There is never a day when you go out to the practice field and everyone is hale and hearty.[17]

UPSETS

There are strategic upsets and psychological upsets. Ours were psychological upsets.[18]

— referring to Northwestern's numerous upsets while coaching there, including victories over Ohio State, Michigan, and Notre Dame (four times)

Ara: Season by Season

1951

Miami (Ohio), 7-3

Date	Opponent	Site	Result	Score
Sept. 22	Wichita	Away	W	21-13
Sept. 29	Bowling Green	Home	W	46-7
Oct. 6	Xavier	Home	L	14-32
Oct. 13	Western Michigan	Away	W	34-27
Oct. 20	Ohio	Home	W	7-0
Oct. 27	Marquette	Away	L	7-27
Nov. 3	Buffalo	Home	W	27-7
Nov. 10	Dayton	Away	W	21-20
Nov. 17	Western Reserve	Home	W	34-7
Nov. 24	Cincinnati	Away	L	14-19

1952

Miami (Ohio), 8-1

Date	Opponent	Site	Result	Score
Sept. 27	Bowling Green	Away	W	42-7
Oct. 4	Xavier	Home	W	26-7
Oct. 11	Western Michigan	Home	W	55-6
Oct. 18	Wichita	Away	W	56-7
Oct. 25	Ohio	Away	W	20-0
Nov. 1	Toledo	Home	W	27-13
Nov. 7	Marquette	Away	W	22-21
Nov. 15	Dayton	Home	W	27-13
Nov. 27	Cincinnati	Away	L	9-34

1953

Miami (Ohio), 7-1-1

Date	Opponent	Site	Result	Score
Sept. 26	Bowling Green	Home	W	47-0
Oct. 3	Xavier	Home	W	28-6
Oct. 10	Western Michigan	Away	W	52-6
Oct. 17	Marshall	Away	W	48-6
Oct. 24	Ohio	Home	T	7-7
Oct. 31	Toledo	Away	W	81-0
Nov. 7	Tennessee Tech	Home	W	44-6
Nov. 14	Dayton	Away	W	20-7
Nov. 26	Cincinnati	Away	L	0-14

1954

Miami (Ohio), 8-1

Date	Opponent	Site	Result	Score
Sept. 25	Bowling Green	Away	W	46-7
Oct. 2	Marquette	Away	W	27-26
Oct. 9	Xavier	Home	W	42-7
Oct. 16	Marshall	Home	W	46-0
Oct. 23	Ohio	Away	W	46-13
Oct. 31	Western Michigan	Home	W	48-0
Nov. 6	Indiana	Away	W	6-0
Nov. 13	Dayton	Home	L	12-20
Nov. 25	Cincinnati	Away	W	21-9

1955

Miami (Ohio), 9-0

Date	Opponent	Site	Result	Score
Sept. 24	Northwestern	Away	W	25-14
Oct. 1	Xavier	Home	W	13-12
Oct. 8	Toledo	Home	W	47-0
Oct. 15	Marshall	Away	W	46-7
Oct. 22	Ohio	Home	W	34-7
Oct. 29	Kent State	Away	W	19-7
Nov. 5	Bowling Green	Home	W	7-0
Nov. 12	Dayton	Away	W	21-0
Nov. 24	Cincinnati	Away	W	14-0

1956

Northwestern, 4-4-1

Date	Opponent	Site	Result	Score
Sept. 29	Iowa State	Home	W	14-13
Oct. 6	Tulane	Home	L	13-20
Oct. 13	Minnesota	Away	T	0-0
Oct. 20	Michigan	Away	L	20-34
Oct. 27	Indiana	Away	L	13-19
Nov. 3	Ohio State	Home	L	2-6
Nov. 10	Wisconsin	Away	W	17-7
Nov. 17	Purdue	Home	W	14-0
Nov. 24	Illinois	Home	W	14-13

1957

Northwestern, 0-9

Date	Opponent	Site	Result	Score
Sept. 28	Stanford	Away	L	6-26
Oct. 5	Oregon State	Home	L	13-22
Oct. 12	Minnesota	Home	L	6-41
Oct. 19	Michigan	Away	L	14-34
Oct. 26	Iowa	Home	L	0-6
Nov. 2	Ohio State	Away	L	6-47
Nov. 9	Wisconsin	Home	L	12-41
Nov. 16	Purdue	Away	L	0-27
Nov. 23	Illinois	Away	L	0-27

1958

Northwestern, 5-4

Date	Opponent	Site	Result	Score
Sept. 27	Washington State	Home	W	29-28
Oct. 4	Stanford	Home	W	28-0
Oct. 11	Minnesota	Away	W	7-3
Oct. 18	Michigan	Home	W	55-24
Oct. 25	Iowa	Away	L	20-26
Nov. 1	Ohio State	Home	W	21-0
Nov. 8	Wisconsin	Away	L	13-17
Nov. 15	Purdue	Home	L	6-23
Nov. 22	Illinois	Away	L	20-27

1959

Northwestern, 6-3

Date	Opponent	Site	Result	Score
Sept. 26	Oklahoma	Home	W	45-13
Oct. 3	Iowa	Away	W	14-10
Oct. 10	Minnesota	Home	W	6-0
Oct. 17	Michigan	Away	W	20-7
Oct. 24	Notre Dame	Away	W	30-24
Oct. 31	Indiana	Home	W	30-13
Nov. 7	Wisconsin	Home	L	19-24
Nov. 14	Michigan State	Away	L	10-15
Nov. 21	Illinois	Away	L	0-28

1960

Northwestern, 5-4

Date	Opponent	Site	Result	Score
Sept. 24	Oklahoma	Away	W	19-3
Oct. 1	Iowa	Home	L	0-42
Oct. 8	Minnesota	Away	L	0-7
Oct. 15	Michigan	Away	L	7-14
Oct. 22	Notre Dame	Home	W	7-6
Oct. 29	Indiana	Home	W	21-8
Nov. 5	Wisconsin	Away	W	21-0
Nov. 12	Michigan State	Home	L	18-21
Nov. 19	Illinois	Home	W	14-7

1961

Northwestern, 4-5

Date	Opponent	Site	Result	Score
Sept. 30	Boston College	Home	W	45-0
Oct. 7	Illinois	Away	W	28-7
Oct. 14	Minnesota	Home	L	3-10
Oct. 21	Ohio State	Home	L	0-10
Oct. 28	Notre Dame	Away	W	12-10
Nov. 4	Indiana	Home	W	14-8
Nov. 11	Wisconsin	Home	L	10-29
Nov. 18	Michigan State	Away	L	13-21
Nov. 24	Miami (Fla.)	Away	L	6-10

1962

Northwestern, 7-2

Date	Opponent	Site	Result	Score
Sept. 22	South Carolina	Home	W	37-20
Oct. 6	Illinois	Home	W	45-0
Oct. 13	Minnesota	Away	W	34-22
Oct. 20	Ohio State	Away	W	18-14
Oct. 27	Notre Dame	Home	W	35-6
Nov. 3	Indiana	Away	W	26-21
Nov. 10	Wisconsin	Away	L	6-37
Nov. 17	Michigan State	Home	L	7-31
Nov. 23	Miami (Fla.)	Away	W	29-27

1963

Northwestern, 5-4

Date	Opponent	Site	Result	Score
Sept. 21	Missouri	Away	W	23-12
Sept. 28	Indiana	Home	W	34-21
Oct. 5	Illinois	Away	L	9-10
Oct. 12	Minnesota	Home	W	15-8
Oct. 19	Miami (Ohio)	Home	W	37-6
Oct. 26	Michigan State	Home	L	7-15
Nov. 2	Michigan	Away	L	6-27
Nov. 9	Wisconsin	Away	L	14-17
Nov. 16	Ohio State	Away	W	17-8

1964

Notre Dame, 9-1

Date	Opponent	Site	Result	Score
Sept. 26	Wisconsin	Away	W	31-7
Oct. 3	Purdue	Home	W	34-15
Oct. 10	Air Force	Away	W	34-7
Oct. 17	UCLA	Home	W	24-0
Oct. 24	Stanford	Home	W	28-6
Oct. 31	Navy	Philadelphia	W	40-0
Nov. 7	Pittsburgh	Away	W	17-15
Nov. 14	Michigan State	Home	W	34-7
Nov. 21	Iowa	Home	W	28-0
Nov. 28	USC	Away	L	17-20

1965

Notre Dame, 7-2-1

Date	Opponent	Site	Result	Score
Sept. 18	California	Away	W	48-6
Sept. 25	Purdue	Away	L	21-25
Oct. 2	Northwestern	Home	W	38-7
Oct. 9	Army	New York	W	17-0
Oct. 23	USC	Home	W	28-7
Oct. 30	Navy	Home	W	29-3
Nov. 6	Pittsburgh	Away	W	69-13
Nov. 13	North Carolina	Home	W	17-0
Nov. 20	Michigan State	Home	L	3-12
Nov. 27	Miami (Fla.)	Away	T	0-0

1966

Notre Dame, 9-0-1

Date	Opponent	Site	Result	Score
Sept. 24	Purdue	Home	W	26-14
Oct. 1	Northwestern	Away	W	35-7
Oct. 8	Army	Home	W	35-0
Oct. 15	North Carolina	Home	W	32-0
Oct. 22	Oklahoma	Away	W	38-0
Oct. 29	Navy	Philadelphia	W	31-7
Nov. 5	Pittsburgh	Home	W	40-0
Nov. 12	Duke	Home	W	64-0
Nov. 19	Michigan State	Away	T	10-10
Nov. 26	USC	Away	W	51-0

1967

Notre Dame, 8-2

Date	Opponent	Site	Result	Score
Sept. 23	California	Home	W	41-8
Sept. 30	Purdue	Away	L	21-28
Oct. 7	Iowa	Home	W	56-6
Oct. 14	USC	Home	L	7-24
Oct. 21	Illinois	Away	W	47-7
Oct. 28	Michigan State	Home	W	24-12
Nov. 4	Navy	Home	W	43-14
Nov. 11	Pittsburgh	Away	W	38-0
Nov. 18	Georgia Tech	Away	W	36-3
Nov. 24	Miami (Fla.)	Away	W	24-22

1968

Notre Dame, 7-2-1

Date	Opponent	Site	Result	Score
Sept. 21	Oklahoma	Home	W	45-21
Sept. 28	Purdue	Home	L	22-37
Oct. 5	Iowa	Away	W	51-28
Oct. 12	Northwestern	Home	W	27-7
Oct. 19	Illinois	Home	W	58-8
Oct. 26	Michigan State	Away	L	17-21
Nov. 2	Navy	Philadelphia	W	45-14
Nov. 9	Pittsburgh	Home	W	56-7
Nov. 16	Georgia Tech	Home	W	34-6
Nov. 30	USC	Away	T	21-21

1969

Notre Dame, 8-2-1

Date	Opponent	Site	Result	Score
Sept. 20	Northwestern	Home	W	35-10
Sept. 27	Purdue	Away	L	14-28
Oct. 4	Michigan State	Home	W	42-28
Oct. 11	Army	New York	W	45-0
Oct. 18	USC	Home	T	14-14
Oct. 25	Tulane	Away	W	37-0
Nov. 1	Navy	Home	W	47-0
Nov. 8	Pittsburgh	Away	W	49-7
Nov. 15	Georgia Tech	Away	W	38-20
Nov. 22	Air Force	Home	W	13-6
Cotton Bowl:				
Jan. 1	Texas	Dallas	L	17-21

1970

Notre Dame, 10-1

Date	Opponent	Site	Result	Score
Sept. 19	Northwestern	Away	W	35-14
Sept. 26	Purdue	Home	W	48-0
Oct. 3	Michigan State	Away	W	29-0
Oct. 10	Army	Home	W	51-10
Oct. 17	Missouri	Away	W	24-7
Oct. 31	Navy	Philadelphia	W	56-7
Nov. 7	Pittsburgh	Home	W	46-14
Nov. 14	Georgia Tech	Home	W	10-7
Nov. 21	LSU	Home	W	3-0
Nov. 28	USC	Away	L	28-38
Cotton Bowl:				
Jan.1	Texas	Dallas	W	24-11

1971

Notre Dame, 8-2

Date	Opponent	Site	Result	Score
Sept. 18	Northwestern	Home	W	50-7
Sept. 25	Purdue	Away	W	8-7
Oct. 2	Michigan State	Home	W	14-2
Oct. 9	Miami (Fla.)	Away	W	17-0
Oct. 16	North Carolina	Home	W	16-0
Oct. 23	USC	Home	L	14-28
Oct. 30	Navy	Home	W	21-0
Nov. 6	Pittsburgh	Away	W	56-7
Nov. 13	Tulane	Home	W	21-7
Nov. 20	LSU	Away	L	8-28

1972

Notre Dame, 8-3

Date	Opponent	Site	Result	Score
Sept.23	Northwestern	Away	W	37-0
Sept. 30	Purdue	Home	W	35-14
Oct. 7	Michigan State	Away	W	16-0
Oct. 14	Pittsburgh	Home	W	42-16
Oct. 21	Missouri	Home	L	26-30
Oct. 28	TCU	Home	W	21-0
Nov. 4	Navy	Philadelphia	W	42-23
Nov. 11	Air Force	Away	W	21-7
Nov. 18	Miami (Fla.)	Home	W	20-17
Dec. 2	USC	Away	L	23-45
Orange Bowl:				
Jan. 1	Nebraska	Miami	L	6-40

1973

Notre Dame, 11-0

Date	Opponent	Site	Result	Score
Sept. 22	Northwestern	Home	W	44-0
Sept. 29	Purdue	Away	W	20-7
Oct. 6	Michigan State	Home	W	14-10
Oct. 13	Rice	Away	W	28-0
Oct. 20	Army	Away	W	62-3
Oct. 27	USC	Home	W	23-14
Nov. 3	Navy	Home	W	44-7
Nov. 10	Pittsburgh	Away	W	31-10
Nov. 22	Air Force	Home	W	48-15
Dec. 1	Miami (Fla.)	Away	W	44-0
Sugar Bowl:				
Dec. 31	Alabama	New Orleans	W	24-23

1974

Notre Dame, 10-2

Date	Opponent	Site	Result	Score
Sept. 9	Georgia Tech	Away	W	31-7
Sept. 21	Northwestern	Away	W	49-3
Sept. 28	Purdue	Home	L	20-31
Oct. 5	Michigan State	Away	W	19-14
Oct. 12	Rice	Home	W	10-3
Oct. 19	Army	Home	W	48-0
Oct. 26	Miami (Fla.)	Home	W	38-7
Nov. 2	Navy	Philadelphia	W	14-6
Nov. 16	Pittsburgh	Home	W	14-10
Nov. 23	Air Force	Home	W	38-0
Nov. 30	USC	Away	L	24-55
Orange Bowl:				
Jan. 1	Alabama	Miami	W	13-11

Ara:
By the Numbers

1 Number of times Notre Dame was shut out under Parseghian (0-0 tie vs. Miami, 1965).

2 Notre Dame losses by 30 or more points out of his 116 games: 40-6 to Nebraska in the 1973 Orange Bowl and 55-24 to Southern Cal in 1974.

3 Bowl victories out of five tries: over Texas in the 1971 Cotton Bowl, and Alabama in both the 1973 Sugar Bowl and 1975 Orange Bowl.

4 Number of his Notre Dame players eventually picked first or second overall in the NFL Draft: T George Kunz (2, 1969, Atlanta), DT Mike McCoy (2, 1970, Green Bay), DE Walt Patulski (1, 1972, Buffalo); and DT Steve Niehaus (2, 1976, Seattle).

5 Number of seasons in which Notre Dame under Ara earned at least one national-title mention; in addition to the official title seasons of 1966 and 1973, the Irish also got No. 1 mentions in 1964, 1967 and 1970.

6 Turnovers lost by top-ranked Texas in the 1971 Cotton Bowl, a 24-11 victory for the Irish.

7 Uniform number worn by Heisman Trophy-winning quarterback John Huarte in 1964.

8 Overall pick at which end Jack Snow was taken by Minnesota in the 1965 NFL Draft, Ara's first first-round pick at Notre Dame.

9 Top-10 finishes in Associated Press poll out of his 11 seasons with the Irish.

10 Victories over top-10 opponents while at Notre Dame (10-9-3 overall).

11 Most games won in one season, with the Irish in 1973 (11-0).

12 Number of times his Irish teams scored 50 or more points in a game.

13 Round in which Parseghian, who played at Miami (Ohio), was picked in the 1947 NFL Draft by the Pittsburgh Steelers.

14 Number of years he worked as a network TV college football commentator following his retirement from Notre Dame (seven years each with ABC and CBS).

15 Most points surrendered in one game in the perfect national championship season of 1973, a 48-15 victory over Air Force.

16 Most touchdown passes in a season by one of his Notre Dame quarterbacks – John Huarte in 1964 and Joe Theismann in 1970.

17 Total losses in his eleven seasons at Notre Dame.

18 Number of plays run in an 80-yard touchdown drive that set the tone in the Irish's 51-0 victory over USC in 1966 that concluded a 9-0-1 national-title season.

19 Length in yards of Bob Thomas's decisive field goal in the 24-23 victory over Alabama in the 1973 Sugar Bowl.

20th November date in 1964 that Ara appeared on the cover of *Time* magazine, with a banner that said, "The Fighting Irish Fight Again."

21 Number of Notre Dame head football coaches who preceded Parseghian.

22 Passes thrown in 1965 game by Purdue QB Bob Griese, who completed 19 for 283 yards and three touchdowns in a 25-21 upset of the No. 1-ranked Irish.

23 Length of Southern Cal's unbeaten streak that Notre Dame broke in beating the Trojans, 23-14, en route to a perfect 11-0 season and the 1973 national title.

24 Number of victories for Ara's Miami (Ohio) teams (out of 27 games, to also include a tie, for a .907 winning percentage) in his last three seasons there.

25 Uniform number Parseghian wore as a basketball player at Miami (Ohio).

26 Age at which Ara was forced to retire as a pro football player because of injuries.

27 One of the uniform numbers worn by his son, Mike, as a Notre Dame reserve halfback. He also wore 5.

28 Uniform number worn by USC running back/kick returner Anthony Davis, whose eleven touchdowns in three games against Notre Dame—1972-74—made him Ara's biggest individual nemesis.

29 Largest margin of victory among four straight victories Parseghian's Northwestern teams had over Notre Dame, 35-6 in 1962.

30 Number of times his Irish teams shut out an opponent.

31 Points Notre Dame scored in Ara's first game as Irish coach, a 31-7 victory over Wisconsin in 1964.

32 Number of years that Carmen Cozza, one of Ara's players at Miami when Parseghian was an assistant coach there, coached at Yale in a College Football Hall of Fame career that included a share or win of eleven Ivy League titles.

33 Parseghian's career receiving yards, on three receptions, for the two years he spent playing with the Cleveland Browns.

34 Largest margin of defeat while Ara was at Notre Dame, 40-6 to Nebraska in the 1973 Orange Bowl.

35 Yards gained on the pass Tom Clements threw to Robin Weber late in the 1973 Sugar Bowl that allowed the Irish to run out the clock in a 24-23 victory over Alabama.

36 Victories in seven seasons as Northwestern head coach (36-35-1 overall).

37 Net yards gained in field position by USC late in the 1964 game because of a holding call against Notre Dame that forced the Irish to punt a second time. The Trojans had to drive only 40 yards for the winning score and a comeback 20-17 victory that denied Ara a perfect debut season.

38 Total points given up by his national-championship team of 1966, an average of 3.8 a game. Six of the 10 games were shutout victories.

39 Victories in five seasons as Miami (Ohio) head coach (39-6-1 overall).

40 Age at which he was named Notre Dame coach in December 1963.

41 Total yards Parseghian had on two career kickoff returns for the Browns.

42 Jersey number worn by halfback John Pont whose senior season at Miami (Ohio), 1951, was Ara's first as head coach. Pont, later an assistant coach under Parseghian, was the first player in Miami school history to have his jersey retired.

43 Age at which Ara won his first official national title, in 1966 at Notre Dame.

44 Where *The Sporting News* ranked Ara on its list of the all-time 50 best coaches, across all sports.

45 Number of years Notre Dame adhered to a no-bowl policy until the school accepted a bid to the 1970 Cotton Bowl.

46 Margin, by votes, of Ara's victory over the runner-up, cartoonist Garry Trudeau, in Senior Class Fellow voting at Notre Dame in 1975.

47 The length in yards of a Dick Kenney field goal that gave Michigan State an early 10-0 lead in the classic 1966 game matching Nos. 1 and 2, in which the Irish came back to forge a 10-10 tie.

48 Most points scored by one of Ara's Notre Dame teams in a nationally televised game, a 48-15 victory over Air Force in 1973.

49 Second-half points scored by Southern Cal while storming back to beat Notre Dame, 55-24, in 1974.

'50 Year of Ara's first season as a coach, starting out as freshman coach at Miami (Ohio).

51 Victories for Ara at Notre Dame Stadium as Notre Dame head coach (51-6-1 overall).

52 Combined margin of victory when Parseghian's 1958 Northwestern team swept Big 10 powers Michigan (55-24) and Ohio State (21-0).

53 Age at which Ara coached his last game, as head coach of the College All-Stars, which lost to the Pittsburgh Steelers in the 1976 College All-Star Game.

'54 Year of graduation from Miami (Ohio) for Tom Pagna, one of Ara's star players and later one of his best-known assistant coaches, who also was elected to the Miami Athletic Hall of Fame.

55 Number of times Notre Dame players earned All-America honors under Ara.

56 Length in return yards of Parseghian's lone pro football interception, with Cleveland.

57 Total points scored by Ara's 0-9 Northwestern team in 1957.

58 Overall career losses for Parseghian to go with his 170 career victories.

'59 Season in which he reached his first coaching milestone, his 50th victory, 14-10 over Iowa, while at Northwestern.

60 Uniform number worn by linebacker Jim Carroll, Parseghian's first captain at Notre Dame, in 1964.

61 Uniform number worn by linebacker Jim Lynch, who won the Maxwell Award as nation's top college football player in 1966.

'62 Season in which a Parseghian team reached No. 1 for the first time, getting there by virtue of a 35-6 victory over Notre Dame that gave the Wildcats a 6-0 start.

'63 Year in which Ara's Northwestern team tied a school record that still stands (as of 2011) for takeaways in a game, with eight vs. Wisconsin.

64 Parseghian's largest margin of victory at Notre Dame, 64-0 over Duke in 1966.

65 Approximate distance in feet Ara threw the shot put in 1952 at Miami (Ohio), while an unwitting school shot putter watched in amazement, not knowing that Ara the prankster was throwing world-class distance with a wooden ball painted black.

'66 Year in which Parseghian won his first official national title at Notre Dame.

'67 Year in which Paul Brown, Ara's coach at the Cleveland Browns, was elected to the Pro Football Hall of Fame.

68 Seconds left in the 1970 Cotton Bowl when Texas scored the winning touchdown in its 21-17 victory over Notre Dame.

69 Length in yards of Alabama kicker Greg Gantt's monster punt that pinned the Irish near their own goal line late in the 1973 Sugar Bowl, although Notre Dame hung on for a one-point victory.

70 Number Ara wore as a football player at Miami (Ohio).

71 Longest punt in yards by a Notre Dame kicker while Parseghian was coach—Jim Yoder against Texas in the 1971 Cotton Bowl.

72 Uniform number worn in consecutive seasons by Notre Dame All-Americans Mike Kadish (1971) and Gerry DiNardo (1972).

'73 Year in which Ara won his second official national title at Notre Dame.

'74 Ara's last season as a head football coach, which ended with a 10-2 mark for the Irish.

75 Number of seasons of Notre Dame football that had preceded Parseghian's arrival as head coach for the 1964 season.

76 Overall pick in which Heisman-winning quarterback John Huarte was chosen in the 1965 draft by Philadelphia.

77 Most pass receptions in a season by a Notre Dame player under Ara—Tom Gatewood in 1970.

'78 Last year of three in which three of his Notre Dame players would eventually be chosen (albeit three years after he retired) as first-round NFL Draft picks—Ken McAfee, Ross Browner, and Luther Bradley.

79 Length in yards of what turned out to be the Irish's winning drive in the 1973 Sugar Bowl win over Alabama, culminating in Bob Thomas's decisive 19-yard field goal.

'80 Year in which Parseghian entered the College Football Hall of Fame.

81 Most points scored by an Ara-coached team, when Miami (Ohio) defeated Toledo, 81-0, in 1953.

82 Total number of points allowed by his 8-1 Miami team in 1954, one of three straight seasons in which his Miami team surrendered fewer than 100 points.

83 Yards gained by Notre Dame's leading rusher, Wayne Bullock, in Ara's last game—a 13-11 victory over Alabama in the 1975 Orange Bowl.

84 Most points in a season scored by one of his Notre Dame players, Bob Gladieux in 1968 (14 touchdowns).

85 Ara's uniform number when playing for the Cleveland Browns.

86 Uniform number worn by All-American tight end Dave Casper, one of the stars of the 1973 national championship team.

87 Parseghian's 87th victory at Notre Dame, a 49-3 win over Northwestern in 1974, marked the last time he ever coached a game with his team ranked No. 1. (Notre Dame dropped to No. 2 in the next poll despite the victory, then lost to Purdue the following week.)

'88 Last year in which he worked as a TV football analyst.

89 Number worn by All-American defensive end and Ara recruit Ross Browner, the 1976 Outland Trophy winner.

'90 Season in which quarterback Joe Montana won his fourth Super Bowl ring, with San Francisco, tying him with Rocky Bleier for most Super Bowl rings won by one of Parseghian's former Notre Dame players.

91 School-record number of running plays Notre Dame ran against Navy in 1969, good for 597 rushing yards in a 47-0 Irish victory.

92 Length in yards of an interception return for a touchdown by Nick Rassas against Northwestern in 1965, minutes before he then returned a punt 85 yards for another touchdown in Notre Dame's 38-7 victory.

93 Seconds left in 1964 season finale when USC scored a late touchdown to beat Notre Dame 20-17 and deny Ara and the Irish a perfect 10-0 record in Parseghian's first season in South Bend.

'94 Year in which three of Ara's grandchildren were diagnosed with Niemann-Pick Type C disease, changing the course of his and his family's lives forever as they formed the Ara Parseghian Medical Research Foundation and have relentlessly worked to raise millions of dollars toward a cure for the fatal disease.

95 Total victories for Parseghian in his eleven seasons at Notre Dame (95-17-4 overall).

Resources

I. Ara: His Own Self

1. William Furlong, publication unknown.
2. *Akron Beacon-Journal*, December 1, 1964.
3. Ibid.
4. *Los Angeles Times*, exact date unknown, 1974.
5. Pagna, Tom, with Bob Best, *Era of Ara*. South Bend, Indiana: Diamond Communications, 1976, p. 175.
6. William Furlong, publication unknown.
7. Publication unknown, February 19, 1964.
8. *Sport Magazine*, November 1967.
9. *South Bend Tribune*, March 9, 1975.
10. Quotesea.com.
11. *South Bend Tribune*, January 25, 1980.
12. *The Exceptional Parent*, April 1997.
13. *Sport Magazine*, November 1967.
14. *New Orleans Times-Picayune*, December 30, 1973.
15. "The Ghosts of Irish Legends a Part of Parseghian's Soul," publication unknown.
16. *South Bend Tribune*, May 29, 1999.
17. *Youngstown Vindicator*, March 29, 1964.
18. *Los Angeles Times*, date unknown.
19. *Chicago Sun-Times*, October 25, 1975.

II. Ara: Notre Dame Man

1. Dent, Jim, *Resurrection: The Miracle Season that Saved Notre Dame*. New York: Thomas Dunne Books, St. Martin's Press, 2009.
2. *Chicago American*, May 28, 1964.
3. Statement, Notre Dame Sports Information Department archives.
4. *Chicago Daily News*, July 6, 1964.
5. Dent.
6. *St. Petersburg Times*, December 29, 1974.
7. *Akron Beacon Journal*, December 15, 1963.
8. *Notre Dame Scholastic*, November 16, 1973.
9. *Look*, November 2, 1965.
10. *Chicago Daily News*, October 19, 1964.
11. *Chicago American*, May 28, 1964.
12. *Armenian Digest*, June 1971.
13. *Scholastic Coach*, January 1989.
14. *Sports Illustrated*, November 2, 1964.
15. Ibid.

16. *Grand Rapids Press*, September 19, 1982.
17. *South Bend Tribune*, December 13, 1966.
18. Father Theodore Hesburgh essay, "The True Spirit of Notre Dame," publication unknown.
19. "Parseghian Tours Nation for Talent, Friends for Irish," publication unknown.
20. Thinkexist.com.
21. *Chicago Sun-Times*, October 25, 1975.
22. *Boston Herald-American*, circa 1974.
23. Ibid.
24. *Los Angeles Times*, exact date unknown, 1974.
25. Ibid.
26. *Girard News*, April 8, 1964.
27. *New York Times*, Jan. 1, 1974.
28. *Elkhart Truth*, October 15, 1969.
29. *Boston Herald-American*, circa 1974.
30. *Chicago Sun-Times*, December 25, 1974.
31. Ibid.
32. *Boston Herald-American*, circa 1974.
33. *The Magazine of Naples*, February 2005.
34. "The Ghosts of Irish Legends a Part of Parseghian's Soul," publication unknown.

III. Ara: The Coach

1. *Atlanta Constitution*, September 5, 1974.
2. *Scholastic Coach*, January 1989.
3. *Coach and Athletic Director*, January 2007.
4. *Chicago American*, October 29, 1962.
5. *Grand Rapids Press*, September 19, 1982.
6. William Furlong, publication unknown.
7. *Notre Dame Scholastic*, November 16, 1973.
8. William Furlong, publication unknown.
9. *Dallas Morning News*, December 30, 1977.
10. *Chicago American*, November 25, 1965.
11. *Miami News*, October 5, 1971.
12. *Los Angeles Times*, exact date unknown, 1974.
13. *Chicago Sun-Times*, November 6, 1964.
14. *Scholastic Coach*, January 1989.
15. Ibid.
16. Parseghian, Ara, and Tom Pagna, *Parseghian and Notre Dame Football*, Notre Dame, Indiana: Men-in-Motion, p. xiii.
17. *South Bend Tribune*, November 29, 2009.
18. "Parseghian Tours Nation for Talent, Friends for Irish," publication unknown.
19. *Chicago Daily News*, exact date unknown, 1958.
20. *Elkhart Truth*, October 20,

1970.
21. Parseghian letter to Edwin Pope, February 11, 1986.
22. *Scholastic Coach*, January 1989.
23. *United Mainliner*, October 1965.
24. *South Bend Tribune*, November 29, 2009.
25. *Scholastic Coach*, January 1989.
26. *Boston Herald-American*, circa 1974.
27. *Chicago Sun-Times*, date unknown.
28. Parseghian and Pagna.
29. *Chicago America*, June 2, 1967.
30. *Niles Daily Star*, September 28, 1971.
31. *Cincinnati Enquirer*, February 15, 1975.
32. *South Bend Tribune*, December 27, 1970.
33. *The Magazine of Naples*, February 2005.
34. Dent, Jim, *Resurrection*.
35. Ibid.
36. *Chicago Sun-Times*, date unknown.
37. Phillips, Bob, "Straight As an Ara," *Scholastic Coach*, January 1989.
38. *Grand Rapids Press*, September 19, 1982.
39. *South Bend Tribune*, November 29, 2009.
40. *Boston Herald-American*, circa 1974.
41. William Furlong, publication unknown.
42. *New York Times*, January 8, 1964.
43. *Scholastic Coach*, January 1989.
44. *New York Daily News*, September 5, 1974.

IV. Ara: His Players

1. "Parseghian Tours Nation for Talent, Friends for Irish," publication unknown.
2. Rev. Theodore Hesburgh essay, "The True Spirit of Notre Dame," publication unknown.
3. *Scholastic Coach*, January 1989.
4. *Atlanta Constitution*, September 5, 1974.
5. *Sport Magazine*, November 1967.
6. William Furlong, publication unknown.
7. Pagna, Tom, with Bob Best, *Era of Ara*. South Bend, Indiana: Diamond Communications, 1976, p. 20.
8. Thinkexist.com.
9. *Chicago Tribune*, November 3, 1964.
10. *Chicago Tribune*, September 13, 1972.
11. *South Bend Tribune*, September 9, 1969.
12. *Washington Post*, October 29, 1964.
13. *Sports Illustrated*, November 2, 1964.
14. *South Bend Tribune*, May 29, 1999.
15. William Furlong, publication unknown.

16. *Chicago Daily News*, 1958, exact date unknown.
17. *Chicago Sun-Times*, August 3, 1969.
18. Bill Furlong, "Can the Notre Dame Surge Continue?" publication unknown.
19. *Look*, November 2, 1965.
20. "Parseghian Tours Nation for Talent, Friends for Irish."
21. Publication unknown.
22. Delsohn, Steve, *Talking Irish: The Oral History of Notre Dame Football*. New York: Perennial, 1998, p. 151.
23. Jerome Holtzman, publication unknown, November 19, 1968.

V. Ara: The Motivator

1. Irishlegends.com.
2. Pagna, Tom, with Bob Best, *Era of Ara*. South Bend, Indiana: Diamond Communications, 1976, p. 176.
3. *N.U. Alumni News*, January 1958.
4. *Chicago American*, October 29, 1962.
5. *Elburn* (Ill.) *Herald*, May 18, 1961.
6. *The Sales Executive*, April 13, 1971.
7. *South Bend Tribune*, May 29, 1999.
8. *Chicago Sun-Times*, November 23, 1973.
9. *South Bend Tribune*, May 29, 1999.
10. Pagna and Best, p. 113.
11. *Chicago Daily News*, 1958 (exact date unknown).
12. *Chicago Tribune*, July 11, 1976.
13. *Coach and Athletic Director*, February 2003.
14. Thinkexist.com.
15. Delsohn, Steve, *Talking Irish: The Oral History of Notre Dame Football*. New York: Perennial, 1998, p. 159.
16. *Chicago Tribune*, July 11, 1976.
17. *Parseghian and Notre Dame Football*, p. 6.
18. Pagna and Best, p. 12.
19. *Elkhart Truth*, October 28, 1964.
20. William Furlong, publication unknown.
21. Ibid.
22. "Parseghian Tours Nation for Talent, Friends for Irish," publication unknown.
23. Dent, Jim, *Resurrection*.
24. *Chicago Tribune*, December 29, 1977.
25. William Furlong, publication unknown.
26. Ibid.
27. *Farm Progress Magazine*, date unknown.
28. Delsohn, p. 173.
29. *Chicago Tribune*, January 22, 1995.
30. Pagna and Best, p. 56.
31. Ibid., p.163
32. Motivateus.com.

33. Pagna and Best, p. 96.
34. *The Sales Executive*, April 13, 1971.
35. *Chicago American*, October 29, 1962.
36. *South Bend Tribune*, May 29, 1999.
37. Pagna and Best, p. 47.
38. *Family Weekly Review*, September 15, 1963.
39. *Boston Herald-American*, circa 1974.
40. *New Orleans Times-Picayune*, December 30, 1973.
41. *Chicago Tribune*, September 14, 1979.

VI. Ara: Polls, Bowls, and Big Games

1. *South Bend Tribune*, exact date unknown, 1969.
2. Multiple sources.
3. *South Bend Tribune*, January 4, 1965.
4. Thinkexist.com.
5. *Sports Illustrated*, November 28, 1966.
6. William Brashler article, "Ara in the Afternoon," publication unknown.
7. *Scholastic Coach*, January 1989.
8. Garner, Joe, *Echoes of Notre Dame Football: Great and Memorable Moments of the Fighting Irish*. Naperville, Illinois: Sourcebooks, p. 57.
9. *Chicago Tribune*, October 2, 1975.
10. *Fort Wayne News Sentinel*, date unknown.
11. *Sports Illustrated*, November 28, 1966.
12. *SportDetroit*, November 2001.
13. Garner, p. 57.
14. *Chicago Sun-Times*, November 30, 1966.
15. Pagna, Tom, with Bob Best, *Era of Ara*. South Bend, Indiana: Diamond Communications, 1976, p. 19.
16. *Dallas Morning News*, December 30, 1977.
17. *South Bend Tribune*, January 3, 1971.
18. *Akron Beacon-Journal*, December 15, 1963.
19. Ibid.
20. *Chicago Tribune*, date unknown.
21. *Chicago Tribune*, September 3, 1992.
22. *Chicago Tribune*, October 2, 1975.
23. *Fort Wayne News Sentinel*, January 2, 1975.
24. *Cincinnati Enquirer*, February 15, 1975.
25. "At Notre Dame—Think Positive!" publication unknown.
26. Joe Soucherny, 1974 article, source unknown.
27. *Cincinnati Enquirer*, December 13, 1973.
28. *Chicago Tribune*, January 3, 1970.
29. *Los Angeles Times*, exact date unknown, 1974.
30. *Chicago Tribune*, January 3, 1970.

31. *Elkhart Truth*, October 20, 1970.
32. *Chicago Tribune*, September 25, 1973.
33. *South Bend Tribune*, January 3, 1975.
34. *Los Angeles Times*, December 1, 1974.

VII. Ara: With Feeling

1. Pagna, Tom, with Bob Best, *Era of Ara*. South Bend, Indiana: Diamond Communications, 1976, p. 9.
2. *Family Weekly Review*, September 15, 1963.
3. *Chicago Tribune*, July 11, 1976.
4. Joe Soucherny, 1974 article, source unknown.
5. *Chicago Tribune*, September 14, 1979.
6. *Los Angeles Times*, exact date unknown, 1974.
7. *Boston Herald-American*, circa 1974.
8. *Cincinnati Enquirer*, February 15, 1975.
9. *Detroit Free Press*, January 1971.
10. David Israel article, publication and date unknown.
11. *Chicago Tribune*, September 3, 1992.
12. *Chicago Tribune*, September 14, 1979.
13. William Brashler article, "Ara in the Afternoon," publication unknown.
14. Content.usatoday.com.
15. *Sidelines*, Winter 1997.
16. *The Magazine of Naples*, February 2005.
17. *Chicago Tribune*, January 22, 1995.
18. *Mature Lifestyles* (Fort Myers, Florida), March 1997.
19. *Mature Lifestyles* (Fort Myers, Florida), March 1997.

VIII. Ara: Keeping It Real

1. *Boston American-Herald*, date unknown.
2. Skip Myslenski, "Spoiled Sports," *Chicago Tribune*, date unknown.
3. William Brashler, "Ara in the Afternoon," publication unknown.
4. *Chicago Sun-Times*, reprinted in the *Indianapolis Star*, August 4, 1981.
5. Garner, Joe, *Echoes of Notre Dame Football: Great and Memorable Moments of the Fighting Irish*. Naperville, Illinois: Sourcebooks, p. xix.
6. *Sport Magazine*, December 1974.
7. Skip Myslenski, "Spoiled Sports."
8. Ibid.
9. *Indianapolis Star*, October 29, 1974.
10. *Chicago Sun-Times*, October 25, 1975.
11. *St. Petersburg Times*, December 29, 1974.
12. *Chicago Sun-Times*, February 25, 1957.
13. *Chicago Sun-Times*, January 9, 1964.

14. *Chicago Tribune*, November 16, 1970.
15. *Chicago Tribune*, December 29, 1977.

IX. Ara: His Humor

1. *Cincinnati Enquirer*, December 13, 1973.
2. *Chicago American*, October 29, 1962.
3. *Chicago Daily News*, August 21, 1965.
4. Vic Dorr, "Parseghian Abandons Cautious Style," publication unknown.
5. *Chicago Tribune*, April 3, 1964.
6. "The Ghosts of Irish Legends a Part of Parseghian's Soul," publication unknown.
7. Associated Press, September 10, 1975.
8. *Life*, November 2, 1959.
9. *Chicago Tribune*, September 3, 1992.
10. "Parseghian Tours Nation for Talent, Friends for Irish," publication unknown.
11. *Dallas Morning News*, December 30, 1977.
12. *Los Angeles Times*, exact date unknown, 1974.
13. *New York Times*, January 2, 1971.
14. *Elkhart Truth*, April 29, 2001.
15. *Girard News*, April 8, 1964.
16. *Niles* (Mich.) *Daily Star*, September 28, 1971.
17. *The Magazine of Naples*, February 2005.
18. *Chicago Tribune*, July 11, 1976.
19. *Life*, November 2, 1959.
20. *Coach and Athletic Director*, August 2007.
21. Pagna, Tom, with Bob Best, *Era of Ara*. South Bend, Indiana: Diamond Communications, 1976, p. 28.
22. Ibid., p. 266.

X. Ara: His Resignation

1. *Chicago Daily News*, December 18, 1974.
2. William Brashler, "Ara in the Afternoon," publication unknown.
3. *St. Petersburg Times*, December 29, 1974.
4. *Chicago Tribune*, September 14, 1979.
5. *Chicago Daily News*, December 18, 1974.
6. *Miami Herald*, December 27, 1974.
7. Ibid.
8. Tom Callahan, "The Job, Not USC, Forced Ara's Quitting," publication unknown.
9. Bill Scholl, "A Legend Stays in Style," *Today in Michiana*, date unknown.
10. *Chicago Tribune*, December 18, 1974.
11. Brashler.
12. *The Magazine of Naples*, February 2005.
13. *Cincinnati Enquirer*, February 15, 1975.

14. *Chicago Tribune*, September 14, 1979.
15. *Chicago Sun-Times*, October 25, 1975.
16. *Grand Rapids Press*, September 19, 1982.
17. *Chicago Tribune*, January 20, 1978.
18. "The Ghosts of Irish Legends a Part of Parseghian's Soul," publication unknown.
19. *Fort Wayne News Sentinel*, December 17, 1975.

XI. Ara: This and That

1. Thinkexist.com.
2. *Chicago Sun-Times*, reprinted in the *Indianapolis Star*, August 4, 1981.
3. *Philadelphia Daily Bulletin*, October 28, 1966.
4. *South Bend Tribune*, August 31, 1998.
5. *Chicago Daily News*, October 29, 1962.
6. *Journal Herald*, date unknown.
7. Edgar Munzel, publication unknown, November 14, 1967.
8. *Chicago Tribune*, July 28, 1975.
9. *Chicago Tribune*, September 14, 1979.
10. *Chicago American*, October 29, 1962.
11. Pagna, Tom, with Bob Best, *Era of Ara*. South Bend, Indiana: Diamond Communications, 1976, p. 31.
12. *Chicago American*, November 25, 1965.
13. *Los Angeles Times*, exact date unknown, 1974.
14. Pagna and Best, p. 109.
15. *Boston Herald-American*, date unknown.
16. Garner, Joe, *Echoes of Notre Dame Football: Great and Memorable Moments of the Fighting Irish*. Naperville, Illinois: Sourcebooks, p. xix.
17. Jerome Holtzman, Associated Press, November 19, 1968.
18. William Furlong, publication unknown.

THE AUTHOR

Compiling author Mike "Monte" Towle is a 1978 graduate of the University of Notre Dame, where he worked four years as a student assistant in the sports information department under Roger Valdiserri, Bob Best, and John Heisler. He also was a sportscaster with student radio station WSND and a sports columnist for the student newspaper *The Observer*. He was a freshman when Ara Parseghian coached his last season at Notre Dame. Towle is a longtime sportswriter whose beats included covering college and pro football for the *Fort Worth Star-Telegram* and *The National*. He is the author of more than 15 books, including works on football legends Pat Tillman, Walter Payton, Vince Lombardi, Johnny Unitas, Roger Staubach, Woody Hayes, and Lou Holtz. Towle lives in Hendersonville, Tennessee, with his wife Holley and son Andrew.